Always A Pleasure

RITA SANDERS

AuthorHouse™ UK Ltd.
500 Avebury Boulevard
Central Milton Keynes, MK9 2BE
www.authorhouse.co.uk
Phone: 08001974150

First published by AuthorHouse 5/25/2010

ISBN: 978-1-4490-5175-4 (sc)

This book is printed on acid-free paper.

authorHOUSE®

This book is dedicated,
firstly, to my mum and dad,
to whom I owe a great debt of gratitude

Secondly, to Samoyeds everywhere
and to all animals.

May they all be treated with kindness
and respect and live safe, happy lives,
free from pain and suffering.

CONTENTS

CHAPTER 1

How It All Started.

Always a pleasure ? Yes, although it is sometimes hard to hold on to that thought. It all started about 27 years ago. By then my husband and I had been married for twelve years, I had expected to have given up work, be living in the English countryside with 2 point 4 children and a dog. I was living in a village in a rural setting but I had not given up work, there were no children and no dog. I cannot remember why we thought that this was a good time to get a dog, but we did.   The next question was, what sort of dog.

As a child I lived at Lesscroft Farm with my mum Althea Elsie (known as Lal) my dad, Richard and my maternal grandfather, Jack Parry, who was the farmer. Lesscroft Farm was set in a small hamlet called Coven Heath which is located in South Staffordshire, part way between Wolverhampton and Stafford and it was actually listed on an Ordnance Survey map. It was a lovely black and white house in a beautiful setting and was both a crop farm and dairy farm. Unfortunately, my grandfather had a heart attack and although he had men working for him, the strain of running the farm was proving too much for him.

The Wedge family (my father's side) were either Land Agents or Solicitors but my dad had decided not to follow the family tradition and became a skilled engineer. At that time he was working for a company that manufactured components for military vehicles and aircraft and was happy with his career choice.

During the war, he volunteered for the RAF but after just one day his commanding officer sent for him and informed him that he had received a letter from dad's employer which stated that he was too valuable an employee and they needed him back. The following day he was discharged and returned to his job, for most of the war years he was a trouble shooter and spent a lot of his time at the Royal Aircraft Establishment in Farnborough. Whilst he loved living in the countryside, a farmer he was not.

Sadly, therefore, there was no-one who could take over the farm and in 1957 we left. After we left, the farm house fell into a state of disrepair and was subsequently demolished. I was a bit surprised at this because it is reputed that Charles 11 rode across Lesscroft land to reach Boscobel and I thought the Royal connection, albeit tenuous, would have saved the house, but it did not.

I have some very happy memories of my childhood at Lesscroft, probably one of the best were the celebrations in 1953 on the day of the coronation of Queen Elizabeth II. We had a huge party for the families of the surrounding villages and the guest of honour was an actor who played Walter Gabriel in the long running radio series, The Archers. He and my granddad, helped by my mum, presented each of the children with a Coronation Crown, a coin worth five shillings, which was a lot of money back then but now equates to only 25 pence. My dad was in charge of the races, the egg and spoon race, the sack race and many more. A thoroughly good day was had by all, life was much simpler in those days.

When I lived on the farm, I was surrounded by animals of all shapes and sizes, from Shire horses through a herd of Hereford cows and a prize winning Hereford bull, down to ferrets and numerous cats and dogs in between. A farm cannot afford to carry passengers, so everyone who lived there had to earn their keep, including the animals. All our dogs were, therefore, drawn from the working/pastoral groups and tended to be on the large side. My husband's family favoured the Boston Terrier and although these are handsome, noble little chaps, they were not my sort of dog.

The discussion began. We registered a failure to agree. We decided to retire to our corners with a book on dog breeds, choose a couple of contenders and meet up later. When we got together for the decision, it seemed that we had, quite independently, come up with the same breed, the Samoyed. Also known as the smiling dog. They originated in Russia, only came in two colours, white and white and biscuit and were bred to pull sleds and guard and herd reindeer. They used to be part of the Working Group, but now came under Pastoral. Neither of us had ever seen a Samoyed, except in books, unless we had made, what I was later to learn would be a common mistake and thought they were 'white German Shepherds' or 'Huskies.'

The next step was to find a puppy and to this end I contacted the Dog Breeders Association who sent me a list of breeders who had a litter of puppies ready for homing. The nearest one to us was about a two hour drive away, so we opted for that one. I rang the number and spoke to a very nice lady who said that her bitch had given birth to four puppies, all of which had been found a home, but one of them had been returned to them. She said that this puppy was female and six months old and asked if we would still be interested. We said yes and she invited us down to her house.

On the Saturday we set off with some degree of excitement at the possibility of owning a puppy in the shape of an adorable bundle of white fluff, at least that was the way they looked in the books. We arrived and were invited into the lounge, we sat on the settee and chatted for a while about the breed, as we talked the kitchen door opened and in glided the prettiest, most beautiful dog I had ever seen. Her coat was pure white with silver tips, her tail like a feather boa carried across her back and the cutest little face. She came over to us and let us make a fuss of her, she then walked across the room and lay quietly under the window.

I thought, what a well behaved puppy for just six months old, then, suddenly, the kitchen door burst open with such a bang as it hit the sideboard, a much larger bundle of white fluff bounded into the room, leapt on to the settee, wriggled about between my husband and myself until we had made enough room for it, then it put its head on my knee and looked up at me with the most soulful brown eyes under the longest white eyelashes. "This is the puppy" said Mrs N. "what do you think ?"

Amazed at the size of this animal, I said "If this is the puppy, who is that ?" pointing to the vision of loveliness under the window. "That is the mother" replied Mrs N   By now I was completely smitten with this puppy, I looked at my husband and he nodded. It seemed that this puppy had gone to a new home but had been returned after a few months, it was not really clear as to the reason for this, all Mrs N said was that the wife wanted a dog, but the husband did not, I guess he got his way.

We agreed on a price, signed a form and just before we left, Mrs N asked if we would like to see the pup's father. She disappeared for a minute and came back with one of the biggest dogs I had ever seen, if it had not been for the beautiful white coat and the fluffy tail carried over his back, he could have been a Great Dane, this obviously explained the size of our new puppy.

We thanked Mrs N for her hospitality and assured her that if we had any problems, we would let her know. With that, we left with our dog and the pedigree papers. My husband drove and I sat in the back with the puppy, she was really good and just lay on the back seat with her head on my knee. Having been out to a new family, they had given her a name but we were not keen on it and thought, a new start, a new name. We had about three hours (the length of time it would take to get home) to think of a new name. Since the breed is Russian, we thought a Russian name would be nice, we finally came up with Zara.

Lesscroft Farm, Coven Heath
My childhood home and the venue for the Coronation celebrations of
Queen Elizabeth 11 on 2nd June 1953

Me with my mum, Lal and my dad, Richard at the
Coronation celebrations for Queen Elizabeth 11 on 2nd June
1953

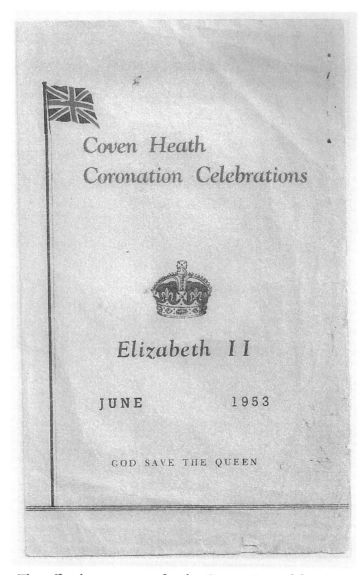

The official programme for the Coronation celebrations
of Queen Elizabeth 11 on 2nd June 1953

First page

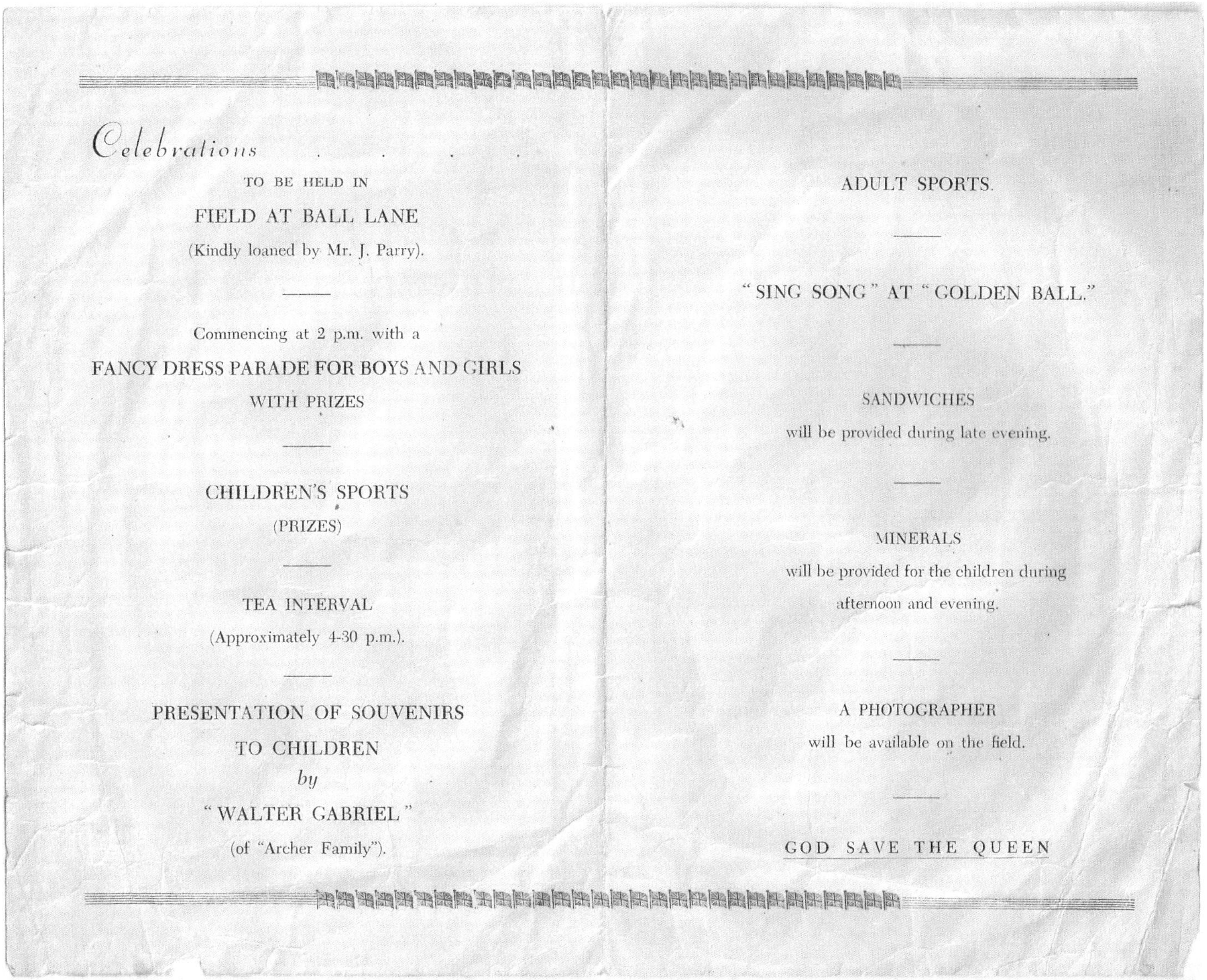

Celebrations . . . . .

TO BE HELD IN

FIELD AT BALL LANE

(Kindly loaned by Mr. J. Parry).

————

Commencing at 2 p.m. with a

FANCY DRESS PARADE FOR BOYS AND GIRLS

WITH PRIZES

————

CHILDREN'S SPORTS

(PRIZES)

————

TEA INTERVAL

(Approximately 4-30 p.m.).

————

PRESENTATION OF SOUVENIRS
TO CHILDREN
by
"WALTER GABRIEL"
(of "Archer Family").

ADULT SPORTS.

————

"SING SONG" AT "GOLDEN BALL."

————

SANDWICHES

will be provided during late evening.

————

MINERALS

will be provided for the children during

afternoon and evening.

————

A PHOTOGRAPHER

will be available on the field.

————

GOD SAVE THE QUEEN

The middle pages

CHAPTER 2

Bringing Zara Home

We arrived home around tea time and took Zara straight into the house, she had a good look round the lounge and kitchen and then went out into the garden. We have quite a large back garden so there was plenty of room for her to run around. She did what she needed to do and came back in. She then did some more exploring and went upstairs into the bedroom, that is where we made our first mistake, we lifted her on to the bed, she shuffled into the middle of it, stretched out and put her head on the pillow. That is where she slept from that day forward. Every night it was a race to see who got the bed first, she always won, of course. When she was little this was not really a problem as she did not take up too much room As she got bigger, however, it did become a real problem as she took up more and more space and it took some hard negotiating to persuade her to relinquish any of it.

On the Sunday morning, we thought we would introduce her to the neighbours We put on her nice new red collar and lead and took her out of the front door, everyone was keen to meet her and she loved all the attention. On the Monday, I took her for a walk round the village, just to show her off, at one point she broke into a trot and I jogged alongside her, big mistake. As we got just in front of the little parade of shops, she suddenly and without warning, changed direction and shot straight across in front of me, I fell over, I think the polite term is I went base over apex and landed in a crumpled heap on the pavement. I got up as fast as I could and just hoped that nobody had noticed.   I walked away fairly quickly and when I got home I realised that my knees were grazed and bloody. I always knew jogging was dangerous, or is it true what they say, pride does go before a fall.

Everywhere we went, she went and always attracted a crowd, a lot of people did not know what breed she was and we were to have the following conversation many times – "Oh, what a lovely dog" "Thank you" "What is it ?" "It's a Samoyed" "A what ?" "a SAM OY ED" "Oh, is that like a Husky ?" "Yes, similar" they seemed to be satisfied with that. Not long ago, I saw a programme on television about Siberian Huskies and in the background there was a Sammy. The narrator spotted this and went on to say that the Samoyed is the refined cousin of the Husky, I am not sure where he got that from. Then there were the other people who rushed over to us all smiles, exclaiming "Oh look, a Sammy, we have one, had one, know someone who has one/had one" we would then spend quite a while discussing the breed. She was also a great attraction for children, they called her a polar bear dog. On one occasion, we were caught in a torrential rain storm and when we got home I noticed that her fur had turned red round her neck. I realised then that a red fabric collar was probably not a good idea and bought a brown leather one instead. This was not the only time that her fur turned red, there would be another occasion which I will come to later.

My husband and I had booked a couple of weeks holiday so that we could be there to make sure she settled in well, she had the run of the house, a box full of toys which she enjoyed playing with and a large garden to run around in. She also liked to carry things and whenever I took her to the shops in the village she would bark and jump up wanting to carry my purchase. One day I bought a magazine and gave her that to carry, this pleased her no end, so from then on, when we went shopping I took an old news paper with me for her to carry back. This seemed to do the trick.

Word had got around that we had this amazing new puppy and we had a lot of visitors in the first week. At this time a lot of our friends were licensees but only one of their pubs allowed dogs. This was still a traditional pub with a posh lounge and a bar with a quarry tiled floor. This is where we went to play dominoes with a group of friends and, of course, Zara came with us. The first time we took her, the licensee gave her a packet of crisps. Every week thereafter, as soon as we arrived, he would say, "go on then, go and choose your crisps" and Zara would go behind the bar, go along the shelf until she found a flavour of crisps she fancied and then put her head in the box and take out a packet. She then lay under the table and ate her crisps while we played dominoes. Crisps are not part of a dog's balanced diet and the eating of them should not be encouraged.

Another of our licensee friends was very fond of dogs and she could not wait to meet Zara, so one night just as the pub opened my husband took Zara to meet her. Already in the pub was one man sitting at a corner table reading his newspaper and drinking his pint. It was not long before he joined in the conversation and said that he had his dog with him in the car and could he bring her in. Our friend said that dogs were not really allowed in, but as it was quiet, it would be OK. He went out to his car and a couple of minutes later returned with his dog and, yes you have guessed, it was a Sammy.

As a result of this chance meeting, we became good friends with him and his wife. He was chairman of a local model aircraft club and invited us to their annual show in the grounds of a stately home near to where we live. When we arrived, there was some sort of technical hitch with one of the model aircraft and he was in the middle of the arena with the microphone trying to keep the crowds entertained. He spotted us and called Zara into the arena, she trotted regally up to him and he introduced her to the crowd. He looked at her and said "would you like to say hello" and held the microphone to her mouth. From the sidelines, in a stage whisper, I said "speak" and she barked into the mic, they had a short 'conversation' much to the amusement of the crowd and then word reached him to say that the problem had been solved and the show could go on. Zara walked out of the arena to rapturous applause.

In the week, my dad took Zara for a walk during the day and I took her when I got in from work. My husband decided that he would walk her at the weekends. He and two of our friends formed a sort of walking club, they looked very like the three old characters from the much loved television series set in Yorkshire. They usually walked around the local area, ending up at a pub. One day, they decided to drive to Wales and walk the dogs up Snowdon. They intended to take the walkers trail but somehow ended up on the track usually reserved for experienced climbers who wore the right clothes and carried the correct equipment, these three had none of these things.

They managed to find their way to the top, more by luck than judgement, but by now they were enveloped in mist and one of the group was so scared, he was unable to move in any direction. The other two tried to explain to him that they had to go down, but he clung like a limpet to a piece of rock and would not let go. My husband, ever resourceful, just happened to have a flask of whisky in his back pocket. He managed to persuade the less than intrepid climber to take a few sips of the Scottish amber nectar which seemed to do the trick. They started the descent but my husband and Zara became separated from the other two. Miraculously, they all made it back to ground level in one piece, but were so traumatised, they had to go straight to the nearest pub to get over the ordeal.

Following that incident, they went back to walking around the local area, but even then, the walks were not always uneventful. Whilst walking along the canal towpath, they heard an almighty splash, turned round to see Zara bobbing around in the canal. Fortunately, my husband is a 6 foot tall, 18 stone, former rugby player and was able to grab her and haul her out.

On one occasion, the Bank for whom my husband worked were playing a charity cricket match against a team of minor celebrities, they were so minor I had not heard of any of them, but we went along to support the teams and took Zara with us, of course. It was quite a hot day and we had taken some water for Zara but unfortunately, we had left it in the car. My husband offered her a few drops of his lager but she turned her nose up at that. The next thing we heard was a slurping noise, Zara had got her head in a glass of dry Martini which belonged to the girl sitting next to us. So my husband had to go to the bar and buy another Martini for her and bought Zara a bottle of water.

Amongst our visitors in that first week were a few of the neighbourhood animals. We live in a small close with about 30 houses and just before Zara arrived a cat called Fred from a house two doors away to the left had adopted us, as cats do and used to sit by the front door until we let him in and then he would curl up on the settee and go to sleep. When we had Zara, the settee, of course, was hers but she was more than happy to share it with Fred, they would curl up at either end and go to sleep. Also keen to meet our new arrival was a dog called Ben who lived four doors away to the right. One day I heard a tapping at the front door, when I went to investigate it was Ben who calmly walked into the lounge, went up to Zara, they greeted each other in the usual way and then went out into the back garden to chase each other around. When they had exhausted themselves running around, they would bark to come in and Ben would walk to the front door to go home. This became almost a daily ritual.

Also on the scene was a ferocious ginger tom cat who hated dogs as poor Ben had found out the hard way. One day Zara spotted this formidable cat and went over to say hello to him, the cat arched its back and Zara stopped, they looked at each other for what seemed like ages, then the ginger tom came over to Zara and rubbed his head under her chin, she licked his ears and a firm bond was created. Their favourite game was chasing each other round a small tree and if we took Zara out in the car and happened to leave the car door open, the ginger tom would jump into the car to come with us. A strange relationship and quite funny to see but not really surprising as Zara seemed to be able to charm anyone and anything.

She was already a huge hit with children and old people because, although she was a big dog, she was gentle and placid. One day we were at an event at our local County show ground, it was a really hot day and my husband had gone into the pavilion to get a couple of pints, leaving me outside with Zara. A few feet away from me were a group of leather clad youths, covered in tattoos and piercings. I got the impression that they were talking about me and for a minute, I felt a little intimidated when a sea of blue ink and black leather surged towards me.

My first instinct was to walk away, but then I decided that they did not frighten me and I would stay where I was. In any event, I knew that Zara would protect me by licking them to death. They got quite close and stopped, all except for one of them who came up to me. "hello" he said, "hello" said I. We then had the usual conversation - lovely dog - what is it - a Samoyed, etc. etc. He asked me "does she bite ?" "Only when I tell her to" I answered with great authority. He then asked if his mates could come over and say hello to her, although I thought they would be better suited to a Staffordshire Bull terrier than a large white bundle of fluff, I said that of course they could. He nodded to the motley crew and they all came over to us. They were polite, chatty and friendly, they all got down on the floor and made a great fuss of Zara, which she absolutely loved. Finally, they thanked me and headed off towards the pig roast. They really were a very nice group of lads. It seemed that Zara had won over another set of fans. Oh and most of them did have Staffordshire Bull terriers !

Zara, like all Samoyeds, was bright and intelligent. I remember one time, after a particularly problematic day at work, I arrived home late and even then the telephone did not stop ringing. Eventually, at around 7 pm, the problems had been resolved and I felt able to relax, sit down and read the paper. Zara, however, had other ideas. Firstly, she kept putting her paw on my knee, then she pushed the news paper with her nose. She continued to do this, despite being asked to go and lie down. Finally, she was becoming a nuisance and I am afraid I got a bit fed up with her antics and shouted at her to go and lie down. Instead, she walked calmly into the kitchen, picked up her dish and brought it into the lounge where she dropped it by my feet and looked up at me. It was then that I realised that, in all the chaos, I had forgotten to feed her. That was the first and only time I forgot to feed any of my dogs.

Zara for all her charm did have another side to her which we would later find out.

Zara when we first had her
aged six months

Zara all grown up

Zara making herself useful

Zara looking in my handbag for a dog chew.

Found one, mission accomplished

Zara enjoying a paddle in the sea
somewhere in Wales

CHAPTER 3

The Dark Side Of Zara

All too soon my husband and I had to return to work. Unfortunately, my mum was not in the best of health and my dad decided to volunteer for early retirement in order to spend more time with her. Coven is set in beautiful South Staffordshire countryside and there are many walks in and around the area, including along the tow path of the Staffordshire and Worcestershire Canal which flows just on the outskirts of the village. My dad had always enjoyed walking and was more than happy to come down to my house every day and take Zara out for a couple of hours, which meant that she would not spend too much time on her own. It became evident, however, that she was not happy spending any time at all on her own.

My husband is not the tidiest of people and would leave his jackets on a chair in the lounge and his shoes on the floor. She became very adept at taking out the insoles of his shoes. She would go through his jacket pockets and shredded his wallet, credit cards and numerous pens. She would then tear the lining of the pockets to shreds. My husband worked in a bank and because of this he was often asked to audit the books of several of the village organisations. Their paper work, which included some cash, came in various packages, one lot arrived in a super market plastic carrier bag, which my husband chose to leave on the coffee table. I was horrified when I came in from work one day to find the lounge carpet covered in bits of invoices, bills, cheques and £5, £10 and £20 notes.

She demolished her toy box, which was a plastic laundry basket, this I found in a thousand pieces all over the lounge floor. She also broke into the pantry and scattered flour, sugar and rice all over the kitchen floor. There were also a few tins lying around with teeth marks in them and she had eaten the labels. Dinner, for the next few days, was quite interesting. Following that incident, we tied the pantry door up with string, it was not very aesthetic but it worked.

One morning the alarm clock woke me up and I thought I would just have five more minutes, so I turned over in bed and felt something greasy with sharp edges against my cheek. I opened my eyes with some degree of trepidation to find my head resting on a chicken carcass. The night before, we had all had roast chicken for dinner and I had carefully wrapped the remains of the chicken in a plastic bag, tied it up and put it in the pedal bin in the kitchen. I forgot to lift the bin up off the floor before I went to bed and she must have got into the bin, taken the carcass out of the bag and brought it upstairs to bed.

Just before one Christmas, she managed to open the cupboard in the side board where I had put several boxes of chocolate liqueurs which I had bought as presents for friends. All that was left were bits of cardboard packaging and silver paper. How she survived is a mystery because, as we all know, human chocolate is poisonous to dogs and I do not imagine that the alcohol did her much good either. The next day her eyes were bloodshot and she was a bit lethargic, I did wonder if she had got a hangover, do dogs get headaches ?

My husband went through a phase of taking photographs and only bought the best of equipment. Unfortunately, he was not very careful where he left it and she destroyed a couple of very expensive cameras. We tried to be more careful about what we left lying around, but this did not always work.

We borrowed a book from a friend, I read it and put it on the bookshelf amongst many other books, ready for my husband to read. One day, Zara was obviously bored and must have climbed on to the settee and put her feet on the back of it to reach the books. Of all the books she could have taken, she chose the one we had borrowed and tore it to shreds. It cost me £16.99 to replace it and it was not even that good a book ! I decided to lay new lino tiles in the hall, it took me absolutely ages but I was very pleased with the result. It was short lived, however, because one day when I got in from work, she had ripped up every single one.

I had noticed that I was getting a few grey hairs (hardly surprising) and was not very happy about this so I decided to try a semi permanent colour rinse to get rid of them. I chose the colour Mahogany which I thought would blend in well with my then dark brown hair. I was pleased with the result and thought it looked quite natural and since no-one had made any comments, I thought I had got away with it. Unfortunately, Zara went on a rummage in the bedroom got hold of what I thought was an empty tube and somehow managed to get a large blob of the colour on the top of her head and all down one ear. Mahogany on white fur comes out as bright red and although it was a semi permanent colour it took ages to wash out, so for several days, she had these bright red patches on her beautiful white fur which I had to explain to everyone who asked. Since I could not come up with a reasonable excuse, I had to tell the truth, so my secret was out. Following this incident, we fitted a bolt on the bedroom door.

After much persuading, my husband agreed to re-paper the hall, stairs and landing. He made a good job of it and was pleased with his efforts. Zara was obviously not so impressed because she tore a good deal of the paper off the hall wall and I found piles of shredded paper all over the floor. This must have traumatised my husband more than I realised because he has not done any decorating since !

It got to the point where I just never knew what I was going to find when I came back, there had been so many instances, but it came to a head one day when my dad rang me at the office. I knew it must be serious because my dad did not believe in personal calls at work, so I waited with baited breath to hear the worst. It seemed that Zara had bitten or scratched or both, a few holes in the seat of my settee which I had only just had re-upholstered and most of the stuffing was all over the floor. My dad had found it when he came down to take her out and he wanted to warn me and not let me just walk in and find it. I really could not go on like this any longer and was at a loss to know what to do.

Zara reclining on 'her' settee

Zara obviously did not like the new covering on her settee

Zara looking so angelic

Zara ripped up the tiles on the hall
floor and a bit more besides

Another toy box damaged beyond repair (Not to mention the shoe!)

CHAPTER 4

The Solution

My friends all thought I was mad to still have her after all that she had done and the money she had cost us, but they knew just how much she meant to me and that I loved her to bits. Despite all that Zara had put me through, I just could not bear to part with her, especially as my mum had also grown so fond of her and looked forward to her visits. My mum by this time was bedridden and Zara seemed to understand that my mum was very ill and so she was really gentle with her. Zara would jump on the bed and lie close to my mum so that she could reach to stroke her. My dad was horrified, dogs on beds !!! My mum really loved having Zara around and that was all that mattered.

It was ironic really that my mum should have contracted, amongst other things, a disease of the lungs. She was a classically trained soprano and had spent hours on her breathing exercises, she could read music and was an accomplished pianist. During the war she joined an entertainment group and sang in theatres up and down the country. She even appeared on the BBC radio programme Workers Playtime.

On one occasion, she was asked to join ENSA but decided she could not as she thought she was needed to help her father keep the farm running. We used to joke about what might have been, she could have been the forces sweetheart and become Dame Althea. It was so hard to believe that this once vivacious, vibrant woman, who had held an audience captive with her amazing singing voice, was now lying in bed hardly able to breathe. Sadly, my mum died in 1986 on 24th August, my dad's birthday.

In order to try to find a solution to the problem that was Zara, I bought loads of 'dog magazines' and read all the vets. articles, breed advice etc. It was in one of these magazines that I came across an advert which said that some dog fur (including the Samoyed) could be spun and then knitted into garments. I thought this sounded like a good idea because Samoyeds have really thick, beautiful coats and it always seemed a shame to just throw away all the fur when they had been brushed. I rang the number and spoke to a very nice lady and we agreed to meet for lunch. She had three Samoyeds of her own and it was through her that we got to hear about the British Samoyed Club. One of her friends was on the committee and she got her to send us details of their next AGM. We thought we would go along and meet other Sammy owners, tell them our problems and ask their advice. Somehow, at the end of the meeting, we found ourselves on the committee.

Everyone was so friendly and made us feel really welcome. They were all more than happy to discuss their Sams and listen to our problems and offer advice. We learned a lot about the breed, including the breed standards, it seems that bitches should be about 19/20" to the shoulder, pity no-one told Zara that because she was now about 23" to the shoulder. My husband and I served on the committee for several years, we had some really good times and met many lovely people but the showing aspect was of no real interest to me.

At one of our meetings, the subject came up with regard to the amount of the donation the Club should give that year to the Samoyed Rescue. I had not heard of the rescue before and was intrigued to find out more. It seems that most breeds have their own rescue society and the Samoyed was no exception.

During all our discussions regarding what to do about the problem that was Zara, the general consensus seemed to be that she was suffering from anxiety separation and maybe another dog as a companion might help. I immediately thought that a rescue Sam would be the answer, it would help Zara and give an unfortunate dog a good home. When I told my friends, they once again thought I was completely mad but my husband and I agreed that we would give it a try.

We rang the number for the Samoyed Rescue and spoke to a very nice lady who was more than happy to tell us all about the work of the rescue. She had been around Sams for many years and had built up quite an extensive network of like minded people up and down the country. The more she spoke, the more I realised that I would very much like to be a part of it. I was really impressed with the commitment and dedication that the rescue had for the breed and the welfare of the dogs. We arranged to meet and I told her the problems we were having and asked about the possibility of us taking on a rescue Sam, I also said that we would like to help the cause and if there was anything that we could do, to let us know.

A short time after our meeting, she received a call from an animal shelter in South Wales to say that they had just removed three dogs from one family, a Jack Russell, a Collie cross and a Sam. They said that it looked as though the Jack Russell had been used as a football as he had such horrific injuries and despite the best efforts of the sanctuary staff, he was in such a bad way that they had to have him 'put down' but they still had the other two dogs. The Rescue rang us and told us about the Sam, we agreed to drive down to South Wales to get him, with the intention of keeping him. Obviously it depended on how Zara got on with him but I knew it would be OK because despite her bad behaviour when we were not around, she really was the sweetest, gentlest dog.

We contacted the sanctuary and agreed a date to go down, unfortunately, the night before the agreed date it snowed really heavily and was still snowing on that morning. It was a four hour journey and it would have been madness to attempt to go that far in such conditions. We rang the sanctuary and asked if they would look after him for one more week. They agreed. The following weekend, there was still some snow around but we decided to take the risk and drive down there. We were met at the gate by the owner who invited us in to the kennels. I could hear all the dogs barking and because I could not bear to see all those pleading eyes, I asked if she would bring the Sam out to us.

She went to fetch the dog and when I saw this poor, pathetic creature, it almost broke my heart, it was hard to believe that he and Zara were the same breed. His eyes were dull, there was no sparkle there, he was grubby and matted and he could barely walk. He was as tall as Zara but was painfully thin, only half the weight he should have been for his size, he was, quite literally, just skin and bone and had very little fur on his tail.

The Sanctuary said that he was 23 months old. They had taken him to a vet when they first got him because he was so underweight, could hardly walk and could not sit unsupported.

They told us that their vet had said that he had most probably been hit by a car when he was a puppy which had resulted in a broken hip that had just been left untreated. As a consequence, it had set wrongly and his one foot stuck out at an angle and he walked with a pronounced limp. He would always walk with a limp and would probably have more problems as he got older. Can you imagine the pain he must have been in, how can people be so cruel.

I knew that I could not leave him there, he needed a lot of love and attention and I wanted to be the one who gave him that and make sure that he had a better life. Zara took to him instantly and I knew that they would be fine together.

Once again, we thought, new home, new name. We called him Max.

Max when he first came to us aged 23 months

Max sitting in his corner of the lounge

CHAPTER 5

Zara's New Companion

My husband had an estate car at that time and we put Zara in the very back and lifted Max on to the back seat. I sat in the back with him and he never moved or made any noise all the way back. We got home, Zara bounded in to the house full of the joys of life, we managed to get Max out of the car and he walked into the house reluctantly and warily. We got him into the lounge and he just sat in a corner (he could only sit if he had something to lean on) and would not go any further. Zara took a ball from her toy box and took it to him but he did not seem to know what it was, let alone what to do with it. She brought the ball over to me and we played with it for a while and poor Max just sat and watched, quite bewildered. When she tired of the game, she decided to offer Max several more of her toys, but he still showed no interest, he just sat there. She gave that up as a bad job and just sat down by him. Eventually, she lay down and then he lay down and she put her head on his paw, he did not seem to mind that, so that is how they stayed until tea time.

The next thing was to get some food into him, we managed to coax him into the kitchen and showed him a dish full of food. I have never seen a dog eat so quickly, Zara had only eaten half of hers but she stepped away from her bowl and let him have the rest, this also disappeared at a great rate of knots. Feeding him biscuits by hand was a very risky business, if I got too close to him, he would growl and bare his teeth, then he would realise that there was food and would make a grab for it, I am amazed that I still have all my fingers.

One day I was making bacon sandwiches, I put the bread on the work surface, turned round to get the bacon off the cooker and when I turned back, the bread had gone. It was as though he was grabbing food at every opportunity because he did not know when he would be eating again. Slowly, he began to realise that food would come regularly, there was enough to go round and he would get his share. He also became a little gentler when he took food from my hand, but it took quite a while for him to stop growling and baring his teeth every time I tried to get close to him.

The Samoyed is not an aggressive breed, in fact quite the opposite, but this growl was definitely a warning to stay away from him. There may, however, be an explanation, remembering what the sanctuary told us about the little Jack Russell terrier that came in with Max, the way he had been 'kicked like a football,' I did wonder if Max had experienced a similar kind treatment and his growling was borne out of fear rather than aggression.

The next battle was being able to take things off him, including food. It took quite a bit of courage on my part to attempt to take anything off this snarling dog, but I felt it was important that I was able to do this. The battle began, but it was one that I was determined to win. Again, it took a while and a great deal of patience but eventually, he would give up things, including chews, willingly. He also gradually learned that playing ball could be quite fun. To get to this stage had taken well over 12 months.

A few days after we had Max, we took him to our vet for a complete check up. The vet agreed with the sanctuary vet's theory that Max's injury was consistent with being hit by a car when he was a puppy, but I still could not help wondering what the real story was. Whatever the truth was, he had just been left to suffer and his hip had set wrongly. There was an operation they could perform, but it would be invasive surgery and there were no guarantees. I felt he had probably been through quite enough and did not want to put him through any more pain and discomfort, so we thought we would leave it at the moment and see how he went. He also needed to put on a quite a lot of pounds because, as the vet agreed, he was severely under weight.

He continued to eat heartily and gained weight, he thoroughly enjoyed chews and dog biscuits. Zara was rather partial to cheese and when I offered a piece to Max he was not quite sure until he saw Zara eating it, then he tried it and liked it, this became his special treat. We took them both for a walk regularly and Max slowly got stronger and was able to walk further but could still not sit without support, so his favourite spot during the day was the corner of the lounge by the door and at night he slept by the front door. It seemed that he always needed to be by a door.

He was encouraged to come into the bedroom but was never happy being in there (unlike Zara who always slept on the bed) so sometimes he would start the night lying on the landing at the top of the stairs but would eventually end up by the front door. Although sometimes when I came down in the morning, I would find him asleep in the utility room. Soon his limp was less noticeably and he could move as quickly as Zara. At the start of the walk, they both pulled heavily on the lead but after about half way, they slowed down. Max walked beautifully by my side but Zara stopped every few inches to sniff something or find something to pick up. She was very adept at finding dead furry creatures and trying to give them the kiss of life.

Max did not bark much at all, only when someone came to the front door just to let me know that there was someone there, unlike Zara who had to let everyone know she was there, but as soon as he saw me pick up his lead, he suddenly found his voice and did not stop barking until we had left the house. One night, however, we had been in bed for quite a while when I was woken by the sound of Max barking. This was unusual and it was the kind of bark that said there is something going on that you should know about. I looked through the bedroom curtains and could not believe my eyes. There were about a dozen horses roaming around the close, one on our front lawn happily grazing, a couple of others on neighbours' gardens and the rest just wandering about. The one on our lawn raised his head, shook it, made a sort of snorting noise and headed off back down the street closely followed by the rest of them. Since I was not sure where they were headed and was concerned for their safety, I rang the police who told me that they had already been notified and the situation was being addressed.

Max also got to like going out in the car, at first he was very wary, as he was about almost everything, but he soon realised that going for a ride in the car could be fun. One day I took the two dogs to a stately home close to where we live. This particular day was the Town and Country Fair, which is something that I enjoy and they encourage people to bring their dogs but have a strict policy that all dogs must be kept on a lead. We arrived at the park and started to walk around, we did not get very far before I realised that two Sams attract twice as much attention as one Sam.

The fair was well attended, as usual, and it seemed that almost everybody wanted to make a fuss of the dogs. Zara loved all the attention and would actively seek it out, Max was completely nonplussed and decided that the best thing to do was to lie down until all the fuss was over. It was soon time to go home and we headed back to the car. Unfortunately, I had a momentary lapse of concentration, which is never a good thing when you have a Sam on the other end of a lead. It was at this particular moment that the clay pigeon shoot started. Zara hated loud bangs and bonfire night was a complete nightmare, she heard the first shot and bolted, yanking the lead out of my hand and taking off like a Greyhound out of trap one. Max and I chased after her as best we could and spotted her going into one of the tents.

We approached the subject tent to see two bemused stall holders who had been minding their own business, looking at a large white dog hiding at the back of their tent under a table. In between gasping for breath, I mumbled my apologies and tried to coax Zara out from under the table, she was having none of that. I got down on my hands and knees and peered under the table, it was at this point that I heard a deep voice behind me say "excuse me, madam, do you have those dogs under control ?" I turned my head to see black, shiny boots, I looked up a little further and saw black serge trousers, then shiny silver buttons. I thought, oh no, not the police.

I stood up to face the member of the local constabulary only to find, much to my relief, that it was the local village sergeant. When he saw the look on my face, he burst out laughing. He asked me if I was having a bit of trouble, I replied, just a bit and asked him to hang on to Max while I had another attempt to retrieve my errant dog. Finally I managed to get hold of her collar and drag her out, by this time quite a crowd had formed and I left in rather a hurry.

Max and Zara
friends from the start

Zara and Max enjoyed playing in the garden once Zara had taught Max
what the toys were for

Max and Zara playing ball in the garden

CHAPTER 6

The Best Of Friends

There was a very obvious strong bond forming between Zara and Max. He was gaining confidence thanks to Zara's constant reassurance and he had put on quite a few pounds, he was now the correct weight for a dog his size. He was a big dog, about 23" to the shoulder, his fur had grown and his coat was now thick and glossy, except for his tail, the fur never really grew back properly but nonetheless he carried his tail curled proudly over his back. He was, indeed, a very handsome dog. Along with his confidence, he was gaining strength and was able to walk without too much trouble, he still limped a bit and his foot stuck out at a funny angle but it did not seem to bother him. We teamed up with one of our neighbours and her little dog, Rosie. We went for long walks along the canal tow path and my two dogs were fascinated with the ducks on the canal and the odd heron standing on the bank.

Max and Zara would go into the garden together and chase each other up and down the lawn. Zara persevered with trying to share her toys with him and eventually he got to enjoy playing ball. Despite having a box full of expensive dog toys, they really enjoyed playing with the middle of a toilet roll. He also liked to carry things around and became a very good 'go-for.' When the morning paper arrived, if my husband was still in bed, I would give the paper to Max and tell him to take it upstairs. He also liked to fetch the evening paper and we would tell the paper boy to stand at the bottom of the drive, wait for Max and then give him the paper to bring in. He would always bring it straight to me and give it up willingly, he never destroyed it. Whenever we had a new paper boy, it was funny to me (although not for the paper boy) to see the look on their face when this great, hairy white dog bounded towards them but they soon got used to him and would make a fuss of him when he went for the paper.

Before we had Max, Zara had waged war on all my cushions, so I had removed all temptation. Since the only damage I was coming home to now was a few shredded news papers and the odd chewed shoe (my husband's of course, so I was not too bothered) I now felt confident enough to put the cushions back. By now Max was able to move from his corner by the door further into the lounge and he could also sit without support. He liked to sit by the lounge window with his head resting on the window sill which gave him a good view of the close and he could see who was coming and going. One morning I reversed the car out of the drive and decided to just wait a few minutes to see what happened. Max was sitting by the window, he turned away and looked at Zara who was asleep on the settee, I waited and watched, as I sat there, Max got up, walked over to the settee, picked up a cushion and hit Zara on the head with it, this woke her up and a tug of war started, as the cushion split in two, I drove off. That was definitely the end of the cushions.

Zara was pretty good at digging holes all over the back garden but Max was better. The holes he dug were bigger and deeper, I kept hoping he would strike oil. I was never really afraid of anyone trying to break into the house from the back because they would never have made it that far, they would have fallen into one of the holes and possibly broken a leg, we knew where these holes were but we still managed to fall into one every so often.

Looking at Max now as a happy, healthy, confident dog, it was hard to remember the skinny, pathetic, frightened creature that we had first met at the animal shelter. Zara was his best friend from the first day we brought him home. When he was frightened, she would reassure him, through her, he realised that going for a ride in the car could be enjoyable, playing ball and fetching and carrying things could be fun and she taught him to 'speak' for a piece of cheese. It was evident, however, from the cushion incident that Max had a mischievous side and I think that Zara was happy to exploit this.

In the corner of the lounge, we had a wooden, free standing television cabinet, the television was on the top, the side cupboards were full of cassette tapes and there was a video recorder on the shelf in the middle. One day I came home to find the whole thing had been dragged into the middle of the lounge, bringing the carpet with it. I have no idea how they managed to do this, I think it must have been a team effort as I could not move it back by myself, I had to wait for my husband to come home. He put the carpet back and pushed the cabinet back into place. The next day, they did the same thing again. Fortunately, the following day was a Saturday, so my husband rushed off to a builder's merchant and managed to buy some bricks that matched the fire place and built a corner unit to house the television and video. That problem was solved.

Having read that Sammy fur could be spun, I had begun to save Zara's fur and now that Max had a really lovely coat, I started to save his fur as well. Soon I had a black bin bag full to the top of Sammy fur and was getting ready to ring the spinner. Unfortunately, Zara and Max got hold of it, when I opened the front door and stepped into the hall, I was, quite literally, ankle deep in white fur, it was also all over the lounge carpet. One of them must have got the bag and then they must have had some kind of tug of war with it and shaken the fur everywhere. It took me ages to vacuum it all up, as you can imagine.

One day we got a call from a theatre who were staging a production of Cinderella and someone had told them that we had two beautiful white dogs that would be perfect to pull Cinderella's coach. As nice an idea as this was, I had to decline. If you read on, you will probably understand why. Anyway, they were sort of stage stars already. My husband and I served for many years on our village hall committee and every Christmas, Santa made a visit. He sat on a chair on the stage with his two little helpers, all shining white (they had been washed and brushed especially for the occasion) and were wearing garlands of tinsel, red for Zara and blue for Max (so that people could tell which one was which !) They managed to behave themselves at these times because we were close by. I am not sure who the children wanted to meet the most, Santa or the dogs.

In the beginning, we thought it would be a good idea to take the two dogs to training classes in a local village hall. Whilst they understood (but not always obeyed) the basic instructions, I really wanted to know how to stop them pulling on the lead. They seemed to enjoy the classes and meeting other dogs and behaved really quite well. Then we came to the last night, exam night. The final exercise was to take the dogs to the end of the hall, leave them in the down position while the owners went out of the hall for five minutes and then returned to find the dogs where they had been left. At least that was the theory.

We duly took the dogs down to the end of the hall and left them there, we walked out of the hall and then we heard a really loud crashing, clattering sound. We rushed back in to see Max bounding across the highly polished wooden floor like that well known cartoon deer on ice having left in his wake a couple of over turned tables and several stacks of chairs. Zara passed the course and gained a certificate. Max did not. They both still pulled on the lead.

Max and Zara playing with the middle of a toilet roll despite
having a box full of toys to choose from

Zara and Max looking oh so innocent

Zara and Max found the bag of fur I had been saving ready for spinning

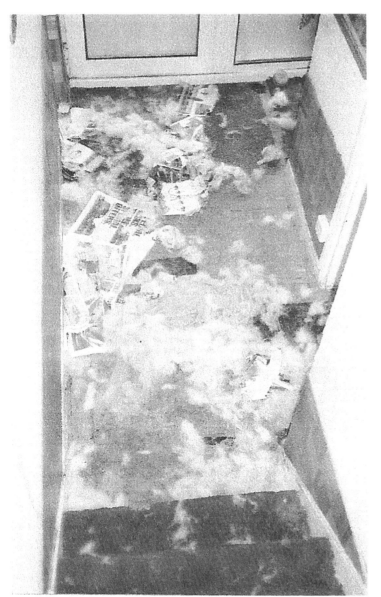

This is how the hall looked

This is how the lounge looked

CHAPTER 7

All Good Things Come To An End

Life rumbled on, the dogs' fame spread. Whenever we saw anyone the first question we were asked was "have you still got your lovely dogs ?" or "how are your dogs." No-one ever asked about us. One day I went to a large department store in Wolverhampton to buy a retirement gift for my boss. As I was buying several items from different parts of the store, all items had to go up to the Customer Service department to be collected and paid for with the one cheque that I had. I did not know the Customer Services lady and I had never seen her before, so when I presented the cheque I asked her if she needed to see my identification. She replied "no, I know who you are, you are the lady with the lovely white dogs."

By now I had managed to collect another black bin bag of fur, so I contacted the spinning lady and arranged to take the fur up to her. The fur came back in neat balls of 'wool' ready to be knitted. I do not knit, although my paternal grandmother, Laura, did teach me how to knit a dish cloth once, but I did not think I was ready to try to knit a wearable garment, so I had to find someone who would. A work colleague did a lot of knitting with mohair and I tried to convince her that dog fur was not too dissimilar to mohair, she finally agreed to have a go.

We decided on a jacket and she did a really good job, we were both pleased with the finished product. I then thought a skirt to go with the jacket would be nice and after much persuasion, she knit me a skirt as well. There was still some fur left over so my husband and I had a scarf and a pair of gloves each. I have only worn the skirt and jacket once and that was to have my photograph taken for the local paper, I am worried about wearing the outfit in case it gets dirty because I am not sure whether to wash it by hand or just throw it in the washing machine like I do everything else.

The dogs got older and we got wiser. Having tied up the pantry door with string, put a bolt on the bedroom door, got into the habit of picking up the rubbish bins off the floor, not leaving shoes and jackets lying about and generally trying to think like a naughty dog before we left the house, life became calmer and they seemed to be happy just spending time together.

When I got up one morning, one of the dogs had been sick. Neither of them looked particularly ill and it was not noticeable from their behaviour which one it was. We went for a walk as usual and just to be on the safe side, I gave them chicken for their tea, which they both ate. The next morning when I got up, there was evidence that one of them had been sick, I let them both out into the back garden and Zara was sick.

A little while later, she was sick again so I rang the vet. We took her later that day and during an external examination, a lump was detected. A blood sample was taken and I had to ring for the results the next day. This I did and was told that there was nothing abnormal in the blood test, but the vet wanted to X-ray Zara and possibly open her up so that they could see exactly what was going on.

I took her the next morning at 8 o'clock for what I believed would be a small operation and all would be well. I was told to ring back in the afternoon around 2 o'clock. At about 12 noon, I received a telephone call, it was the veterinary surgery asking me to go up immediately as the vet wanted to speak to me. Fortunately, my husband was in and we both went to the vets. We were certainly not prepared for the news that was waiting for us when we got there. They had opened Zara up and found a large, malignant tumour in her stomach which was inoperable. Since she was still under anaesthetic, we were told that the 'kindest thing' to do would be to have her 'put to sleep.'

Through a veil of tears, we said goodbye to Zara, a beautiful, loyal and loving companion. Despite all the damage she had caused and the money she had cost us over the last eleven and a half years, I would not have missed a single second of it and I knew that we would miss her dreadfully and I also worried about Max, how would he feel when we returned home without her. When we got home, Max was waiting anxiously for us, he greeted us at the door, just as Zara had taught him. My husband went straight upstairs, I went into the lounge and started to cry, again. I told Max that Zara would not be coming home, he sat by me for a while, then he went back to his spot under the window. He threw his head back and howled. He had never howled before and he never howled again. He had lost his best friend. I had lost my beloved Zara. My first Samoyed.

Jacket and skirt knitted from Samoyed fur

Max and Zara who (unwillingly) donated their fur for my skirt and jacket

CHAPTER 8

A New Addition

During these years we had become more involved with the Samoyed Rescue but retained our place on the BSC committee. We attended all the BSC shows to help out wherever we could. It was at these shows that 'the back of my husband's car' became legendary. Whenever we turned up at a venue, it was almost certain that someone had forgotten to bring a vital piece of equipment. It could just have been a roll of sticky tape or a pair of scissors, a catering size teapot or a bucket and shovel. Whatever item it was, it was guaranteed that one would be found 'in the back of my husband's car.'

It was lovely to see all the Sams at these shows so beautifully turned out, their shiny white coats brushed and combed to perfection. It was obvious that these dogs were loved and well cared for but I was concerned about the Sams that were not loved or cared for and had been rejected for whatever reason. The appearance of these show dogs was in stark contrast to the state of most of the Sams when they came into rescue. Fortunately, my husband and I were lucky as we never actually saw at first hand any case where injury had been deliberately inflicted on any of the dogs. We saw cases of neglect in varying degrees, dirty, matted coats, claws so long they were curling under the feet making it difficult for the dog to walk, dogs that were severely under nourished and some with behavioural problems.

Not all dogs that come through the rescue are the subject of cruelty or neglect. Some of them have been well cared for and much loved but their owners have died and there is no-one to look after them. These tend to be older dogs and are usually a little harder to re-home. Sams get right into your heart and you want to spend the longest time possible with them, but Sammy people are special people and there are some who will willingly take an older dog and enable them to enjoy their twilight years.

My husband enjoys driving and has a very good sense of direction, so he became a driver for the rescue, driving hundreds of miles transporting dogs. I saw my role as more of a fund raiser. Every year the rescue holds a rally, this is a dog show primarily for rescued Sams but everyone is welcome.

The rescue relies on voluntary donations so one year at one of the rallies, I bought a large white teddy bear and decided to do a 'guess the name of the teddy' competition in order to raise some funds. It was a lovely day, the sun was shining and we were all sitting outside around the main arena. I had sold about half of my names when I approached a man with a really handsome Sammy by his side. He dropped the dog's lead to take the list off me and the dog looked at me as only a Sammy can, so I reached down to make a fuss of him when in a split second he grabbed the teddy bear out of my hand and took off round the field with it in his mouth. No amount of shouting by the owner would persuade the errant dog to come back and he expertly dodged anyone who tried to catch him.

Eventually, someone managed to grab hold of him and return him to his owner, but no amount of bribery with biscuits or sausages would make the dog give up the teddy bear. I had visions of having to refund all the money I had collected because the bear would be dirty at best and torn to shreds at worst.

That day, my husband was acting as a steward and was in the middle of a very important class 'The Waggiest Tail' and once a winner had been chosen, he came over to us to find the bear still firmly clamped between the teeth of the dog. One way or another, that dog was going to give up the bear and we devised a plan. My husband looked at me and said "now" he grabbed the dog's jaws and prised them apart, I grabbed the bear, still thankfully in one piece, and my husband clamped the dog's jaws shut and held them shut for a couple of seconds. I do not know who was the more surprised, the dog, the owner or, by now, the crowd of onlookers. I went on to sell the rest of the names and the winner was very happy with the teddy bear.

In addition to the important classes, like the waggiest tail and the prettiest eyes, there were the fun races. It is quite amusing to watch owners trying to run the length of the field whilst attempting to balance an egg on a spoon with one hand and hanging on for dear life to their dog with the other. The most popular race is the sausage race, the dogs love this as they get to eat the sausages. There is a trophy for the winner of each class, all trophies have been donated, usually in memory of a cherished pet, but we tried to make sure that every Sam went home with a rosette. Whilst these rallies are a way of raising funds for the rescue, it is also an opportunity for the rescue to see the difference in the dogs from when they first came into rescue and now with their new owners.

It is also a chance for the new owners to proudly show off their new additions, in some instances, it was hard to believe they were the same dogs. It is amazing what a difference grooming, feeding properly and a lot of love can make. The rallies were always very popular and well attended, they were usually held in the Nottingham/Derby area but people came down from Scotland and up from Cornwall to enjoy the day and meet other dogs and like minded people.

Following the sad loss of Zara, the rescue were the first people we called to ask if there was a Sam available for us. As Max had not had a very good start in life and he was disabled, I felt that with another dog, there may be just too much testosterone, so a female would be more suitable. Unfortunately for us, but fortunately for the rescue, there we no Sams at all in need of a home at that time. This was unusual because most of the time there are more dogs needing a home than there are homes available. We agreed to wait and see if one came through, because you never know when the telephone may ring and there would be an animal in need.

We waited for several weeks and poor Max was really depressed, he had lost the best friend he had ever had, Zara had been by his side for seven years and taught him so much. Everyone knew that we were desperate for another Sam and really looking for another bitch. One of our colleagues on the BSC committee said that they had a six month old bitch which had been promised to someone but that home had fallen through and would we like to take her.

There was still no word from the rescue, so we agreed to go and see her. When we went to see her, we just fell in love with her. she was so little and sweet and very pretty. We agreed a price and left with our new addition.

Tia when we first had her aged six months

CHAPTER 9

Tia's New Home

Our new addition was called Tia (part of her kennel name was Tiara, that is where the Tia came from) obviously we had taken Max down with us when we first went to see her, just to make sure that they would get on with each other. We need not have worried, it was love at first sight for both of them. When we got home, Max walked into the house and we had put a lead on Tia just in case she took off down the road but she pulled me into the house, we took the lead off and she raced around the lounge. I opened the back door and she ran into the garden, had a run around, came back in, went straight upstairs and jumped on the bed. She decided that the bed is where she would sleep and we would just fit in around her, which, of course, we did.

Zara had made herself comfortable on the furniture downstairs and monopolised the bed, Tia did much the same thing, but at least she was a good deal smaller. Max was quite the opposite, he never attempted to get on the furniture downstairs and although he was welcome in the bedroom, he was never really happy in there, he would jump on to the bed when asked to do so but he jumped off almost straight away.

Apparently, when I took Zara and Max for walk, I was a source of amusement being dragged round the village by these two great, white hairy dogs. Although Tia was only half the size of Max, she could still pull quite hard on the lead, so now I was being dragged along by one huge white, hairy dog and one very petite white, hairy dog, which looked just as funny, a bit like little and large.

Tia followed Max around everywhere, wherever he was, she was. She could not just sit by him, she had to lean on him. She looked up at him adoringly and he looked down on her equally fondly. She enjoyed playing with the toys from the toy box and now that Max had been taught what toys were, he tried his best to play but he had only got three good legs and Tia was much quicker than him. He did have his uses though. Tia was happily digging holes in the grass in the back garden but although earth was flying everywhere, the holes were not getting much deeper.

Max was lying on the decking just watching her and must have thought as she was not getting very far, he would help her out. He walked over, nudged her out of the way and showed her how it should be done. In no time, the holes were bigger and deeper, I was still hoping that he would discover oil, sadly he did not. If she ever left his side, he always watched out for her, making sure that she was OK.

At one time, our next door neighbours had a Staffordshire Bull Terrier, who was not the friendliest Staffy bitch I had ever met. She and Tia would stare at each other through a small gap in the fence and one day the Staffy made a really strange growly bark that made Tia jump. Max immediately got up and went over to the fence, pulled himself up to his full height, looked at the Staffy and barked a really deep bark as if to say, hey, you upset Tia and you will have me to deal with.

He was always very protective of her. Trying to be responsible owners, we had decided to have Zara spayed, something about which I felt very guilty. Watching the way she behaved with Max, I think she would have made a really good mum, but I knew that if I had been confronted with a litter of Sammy pups, I could not have given any of them away and, with the best will in the world, I would not have coped with a houseful of Sams. We had Tia spayed for the same reason.

When we picked her up from the vet, she was still a bit woozy from the anaesthetic, so we lay her down on a blanket in the lounge and Max went and lay down beside her. It was not long before she was up and about again and following Max everywhere. I think sometimes, he would have liked a bit of piece and quiet, but he never showed it, he was really very good with her.

We took them to Wales to see the sea, which they loved and had a good run along the beach. On the way back, we called to see my husband's uncle and aunt, who had a sheep farm. The first time we took Zara there, we were sitting talking when we realised that Zara had gone missing. She had managed to squeeze under the gate and get into the field where there were a small number of sheep and was busy rounding them up when we got outside. She had ushered all of them down to the gate by the house and was looking quite pleased with herself.

Sams are bred for guarding and herding reindeer, but, I suppose, in the absence of reindeer, sheep are the next best thing. With Tia and Max, they both just stood at the gate and looked with much interest at the sheep and the sheep stared back at them.

Zara and Max had attracted a great deal of interest, but Tia and Max attracted even more. I think because Tia was much smaller and very pretty, she was a little less intimidating to people who did not know the breed and they really wanted to meet her. Tia, like Zara, loved and encouraged all the attention, Max not so much. He would tolerate people stroking and making a fuss of him but I think he would rather not have been bothered. When he thought that enough was enough, he would move closer to me as if to say, OK, I have done my bit, now can we go.

Tia clung to Max, Max looked out for her. Sadly, Max was getting older, he was now thirteen years old and, as predicted, he had trouble with his 'bad' leg. Arthritis had set in and he was having problems walking, sometimes he would go on to three legs, the vet had given us some tablets which helped, but the problem would only get even worse with age. Even though there must have been times when he was in a great deal of pain, he never complained.

One morning, however, I heard him crying and when I went to see what was the matter, I found that he could not get up. I managed to get him on his feet but he could barely walk and when he did, he listed to one side and could not seem to keep his balance. The vet said that there was nothing they could do for him and that we should consider making 'the decision.' We brought Max home but the crying went on for a few days and I knew that although I did not want to let him go I was keeping him alive for selfish reasons, the time had come. We made the appointment and took him to the vet.

Fortunately, my husband was able to stay with him until he slipped into oblivion, I am ashamed to say that I was not able to do this and had to wait outside. I cried all the way home, for myself, for Max and for Tia. Max was extra special to me, I had spent so much time and effort with him trying to make up for the really appalling first two years of his life and his disability which he bore with great dignity.

There were times, at first, when I thought I would never reach the beautiful dog that I knew lay under the growling, frightened exterior, but I am so glad that I persevered. He had turned into the very best dog anyone could have wished for, from the dog that growled and showed his teeth and would not let me near him to the dog who let me wrap my arms around his neck and cuddle him.

Max was friendly but not effusive. He was not aggressive but proved that he could stand up for himself when challenged one day by a particularly nasty German Shepherd. He was loyal and protective. He would not let anyone get too close to me if I was in my car but it was only recently that I found out that whenever my best friend came over to the house and I left the room for a minute, she was too terrified to move because, if she did, Max would growl at her. He was very wary of people right up to the end. I was the only person who ever got close to him, the only one he really trusted, probably because I had spent so much time with him when we first had him. He never climbed on the furniture and was never destructive. He was intelligent, gentle and sensitive. He was handsome, noble and dignified. He was obedient and respected his station in life. He was very special. He was, in fact, everything a dog should be. He was my dog and I was going to miss him dreadfully.

Poor Tia was distraught, she had lost her mentor and protector, her knight in white shining armour.

Tia with her hero, Max

Tia with Max

Max with Tia in the garden

Max showing Tia that sometimes you have to look out of the window to see who is about

CHAPTER 10

Another Call To The Rescue Society

Poor little Tia needed company, she had clung to Max and now she was alone. The first telephone call we made was to the Rescue Society. They had just re-homed two Sams, so, again, at that time, there were no Sams in need of a home, this was good news for the rescue but not for us. This time my request was not too specific, I thought Tia would get along with either a bitch or a dog, so it was just a matter of time.

Tia had always been a very sweet natured dog, she did not have a vicious bone in her body and apart from pulling on the lead, which most Sams do, taking up too much room on the bed and trying to dig holes in the back lawn, she had no vices, but now when I took her for a walk she would bark frantically at every dog she saw, which was very unusual because she was normally so timid, but as soon as we got up to the dog in question, she just wanted to make a fuss of them. One day when I had stopped to talk to someone, she slipped her lead and ran over to a large yellow Labrador, the dog did not seem to mind although the owner looked a bit concerned, but all she wanted to do was say hello to him. I think she really needed another doggy friend.

She was also becoming destructive in the house. One day when I got in from work I thought it looked unusually light in the lounge and then I realised that a curtain was missing. I looked around the room and found the curtain neatly folded on the sideboard, I opened it up and saw that the bottom had been shredded. I was pondering on this when the doorbell rang, it was my neighbour who used to come over and let the dogs out for me. He explained that when he had come over, he had found the curtain on the floor and decided to fold it and put it out of the way. I could not be bothered at that time to try to find another set of curtains, so he helped me patch the curtain up with some tape and hang it back up. It did not look very aesthetic but it would do until I sorted out another pair of curtains.

The next day, I came in from work early and found that not only had she shredded the curtain further, she had pulled the curtain off altogether and had broken all the tracking. For a few days, I had no curtains up at the window at all. At the weekend, my husband and I went to get some new tracking and another pair of curtains which my husband put up. In order to prevent a recurrence, before I went to work on the Monday morning, I hung the curtains out of the small top windows, I do not know what the neighbours thought. We needed to find a companion for Tia as soon as possible.

We received a telephone call from the Rescue Society to say that a couple were emigrating to Australia and they had a German Shepherd and a Sammy dog called Rushka, which they were not taking with them. It seemed that her parents had agreed to have the German Shepherd, so we agreed to take the Sammy. Time was of the essence for them, so my husband went down to Bristol to fetch him. He was a lovely dog, about the same size as Tia but twice the weight. They were quite different in character, she was quiet and gentle, he was boisterous and bouncy and she seemed quite overwhelmed and a little intimidated by him.

One day, I was in the kitchen when Tia came running in, hotly pursued by Rushka, he pounced on her and she was absolutely terrified. I pulled him off her and she was shaking like a leaf.

I do not think he meant to hurt her, there was no growling or baring of teeth but he did seem to bully her. We learned later that he had lived with this German Shepherd and had indulged in very boisterous play but the German Shepherd could give as good as he got and I think Rushka expected Tia to be the same.

Poor little Tia was just not used to this kind of behaviour and could not cope with it. Perhaps I should have persevered with the two of them but I do not think it would ever have worked, they were just so different and I had to put Tia's welfare first. We rang the previous owners and, fortunately, they agreed to have Rushka back. The last we heard, they had taken him to Australia with them and he was enjoying himself running along Bondi beach.

It took Tia ages to get over this trauma and to stop shaking, she would enter a room very warily and look around before coming in just to make sure that Rushka was not around. We thought long and hard about getting Tia another furry friend and had a chat with the Rescue Society who appreciated our situation and fully understood that we had to send Rushka back but agreed that despite this bad experience, we still believed that we could find her the right companion.

We had received a telephone call from the Rescue Society asking my husband to collect a dog from Wales for which there was already a home waiting but we would be next on the list to get a new Sam. Before my husband left to get this dog, the Rescue Society rang us again, apparently, another breed rescue had found a Sammy bitch on a farm in Wales that they thought ought to be removed from that situation. It was agreed that my husband would pick up both Sams in the one trip.

Whenever my husband was transporting a Sam from one place to another, he would always come home first so that I could meet the dog and the dog could meet our Sams. This trip was no exception, he came home with a large, very handsome but under weight dog and a little, very grubby bitch. The other couple for whom the dog had been earmarked had said that they really did not mind taking either a dog or a bitch and although I had not specified a preference, I really wanted another big dog, what I really wanted was another Max but, obviously, this was not possible.

I looked at this dog, he was two years old and he reminded me very much of Max when we had first had him, except that this dog had four good legs and just for a second I wanted to keep him. Then I looked at the grubby, smelly little creature by the side of him and my heart went out to her, I also felt that because she was in such a dreadful state, I really could not inflict her on anyone else.

She had been kept outside in a shed with straw and concrete flooring with a variety of other dogs. We believe she had been used solely as a breeding machine because her owners had told my husband that because she had only had two puppies in her last litter, she was no longer viable and had to go. They told my husband that she was about six years old, but she appeared to me to be older than that or perhaps she was just worn out. Her fur was really filthy, it hung in matted clumps and the smell was obnoxious and quite overpowering. I have never seen a dog so dirty or one that smelled so bad. We decided that we would keep her and because she had come from Wales, we would call her Sian, which soon became Siani (pronounced Sharnie.)

The new home for the dog was not too far away from us, so my husband put both dogs back in the car and set off. While he was away, I got the brushes out ready but I did not have any dog shampoo because I had always had my dogs groomed professionally, so I was going to have to use one of my bottles of shampoo. When he returned, we brushed Siani in the front driveway. Although I am not house proud by any means, because she was so dirty and the smell was overwhelming, we thought we would try to get at least some of the dirt (and other 'smelly stuff') out of her before bringing her into the house.

My husband then carried her upstairs and we put her in the bath. It took several applications of a well known brand of shampoo before the water was a shade of grey as opposed to black as coal. We wrapped her in a towel and brought her back down stairs where I dried her with my hair dryer and then we brushed her again. By now she was fairly acceptable but I rang the girl who had groomed Zara, Max and Tia and explained the situation. She agreed to groom her in a couple of days, I thought I would give Siani a day or two to settle in with us.

Throughout all this brushing and shampooing, Siani never made a sound, she seemed resigned to whatever life was going to throw at her. She ate the food we offered and then lay down by the kitchen door and seemed reluctant to move, she had no desire to explore the house and was not very interested in Tia.

Poor Tia had watched all this activity and was quite confused and bewildered about what was going on. Tia came to bed with me as usual and my husband spent most of the night downstairs with Siani just to make sure she was OK.

The day we had Siani, Tia did not get too close, with all the washing and brushing, she kept well out of the way. When I got up the following morning, Tia came downstairs with me and went to the patio door and barked to go out. Siani followed her to the door and they went outside together. They did what they needed to do and then wandered around the garden together. They both came back inside and had a biscuit. Tia, like Zara, loved to play ball and she tried to get Siani to play. Poor Siani, like Max, had no idea what a ball was, never mind what to do with it. Whilst Max did eventually learn how to play ball and fetch and carry things, Siani did not, she was just not interested.

Tia looking a bit forlorn when we lost Max

Tia sitting in one of the holes that she dug in the
back garden

All that is missing is the tiara!

Siani when she first came to us and after she had been washed and brushed

Siani says:

First you jump on to the window sill

Then you sit awhile

Finally time for
a nap

CHAPTER 11

The Two Girls Together

Siani and Tia were about the same size, except for their feet. Siani's feet were twice the size of Tia's and I am convinced that if Siani had been given the right diet and had not had so many puppies, she would have been a really big dog. Their coats were quite different, Zara's coat had been soft and silky, Max's coat had been much coarser. Tia's coat was soft and silky, Siani's coat was much coarser and thicker, it was a bit like a sheep's fleece. We took her to be groomed and it was hard to believe it was the same dog. Her coat was brilliant white and you could see the silver tips and, I have to say, she smelled much much better.

We also took her to see our vet for a check up just to make sure she was OK. The first thing he said to us was that she appeared to have had a lot of puppies, but apart from that, she was in good health. She enjoyed going for a walk but did not like having a lead on, she kept turning round and trying to bite it. Unlike Zara, Max and Tia, however, she never pulled on the lead, she was a joy to take for a walk.

Our house is situated at the bottom of a cul-de-sac, the large window with a wide window sill, as Max had discovered, is a good place to sit and watch the world go by and Siani thought so too. Unfortunately Siani was much smaller than Max and sitting on the floor, she could not quite see over the sill. One day, in order to get a better view, she jumped on to the window sill and slid along it like a shot of red eye across a saloon bar, coming to an abrupt halt as her feet hit the opposite wall. This did not put her off, however, so we decided for her safety we would put carpet all along the window sill. I bet there are not very many houses with carpeted window sills. This seemed to meet her requirements and she spent hours just sitting and watching. She never barked at anyone in the street, anyone coming down our driveway or even when someone rang the front door bell, in fact the only time she did bark was when she wanted to go out. Tia would bark if anyone came to the door, she could also tell when our telephone rang. Sometimes, I was not sure if it was the house telephone ringing or the noise was coming from the television set, but Tia always knew.

The girls, as they became known, liked to spend time in the back garden, Tia would play with a ball and Siani would just sit and watch her. We have quite a large back garden which is enclosed all round by a six foot fence and we had a four foot gate at the bottom which leads on to the alley, on the other side of that are fields. When you come out of the gate into the alley, if you turn right it leads to the church and eventually on to the main A449 which is a very fast and busy road. If you turn left in the alley, it leads to the pub (very handy) and then into the village. I thought the garden was quite safe and did not worry when they were out there.

One day, just after we had Siani, I had let the dogs out into the garden and I had then gone into the utility room to do some washing. Every so often, I would check on the girls to make sure they were alright, one time I could not see them and then I noticed that the back gate was swinging in the breeze.

Just as I was starting to panic because I did not know in which direction they had gone, the telephone rang, it was one of the girls from the cake shop to say that she had seen the dogs go past the shop window and one of the girls from the grocery store had gone after them. I grabbed the leads and dashed down to the village, there were two men working on the pub roof and, before I had chance to say anything, they waved their arms and said "they have gone that way." I continued running into the village and more people were telling me that they had "gone down there." Fortunately, Tia had seen someone she knew and had gone up to him and Siani had gone with her. By this time, the girl from the grocery store had caught up with them and they were able to hang on to both dogs until I got there. I managed to get the leads on the dogs and brought them home.

The back gate fastened with a latch and Siani must have pushed the latch up and opened the gate. Tia, bless her, would never have done such a thing but she just followed Siani on her adventure. I rang my husband to tell him what had happened and on his way home he called at the hardware store and bought a large bolt. The kind that slides along and down, which he fixed in place.

The next day, safe in the knowledge that she would never manage to open the gate now that the bolt had been fixed, I let the girls out into the garden. I stood in the conservatory for a few minutes just watching and could not believe my eyes. Siani went down to the gate and looked at it for a couple of minutes, I stood and watched as she, apparently, was sizing it up. Suddenly, from a standing start, she leapt on to the top of the gate, just as I screamed "no" she went over the top. Poor Tia looked quite bewildered as I ran down the garden and into the alley where I managed to catch up with Siani and bring her back. My husband managed to find a piece of wood which he nailed on to the top of the gate, which now made the gate six feet high, it did not look very aesthetic but hopefully it would work. Siani went down to the gate, had a good look but must have decided it was just a little bit too high and gave up. The garden was now Siani proof.

Tia came to us from a home where she was loved and well cared for. We treated her like a little princess, she never had to worry about anything, like where her next meal was coming from or where or how she would sleep. Siani's life had been completely the opposite. I got the feeling that she had lived off her wits and fended for herself from a very early age. She was a 'street kid' but she was very laid back and chilled out. Where Tia was nervous, Siani was calm, nothing fazed her. She was just what Tia needed, I think she made her feel more confident. They seemed to compliment each other and a strong bond of friendship formed between the two of them. Unlike Tia with Max when she had to be with him wherever he was, Tia and Siani had their own space. Sometimes they would lie together and other times, Tia would be in the lounge and Siani in the kitchen, but if one of them made a noise of some sort, the other would find them and check to make sure that they were alright.

Tia was definitely an indoor dog but Siani liked to be outside, I think that is what she was used to. She spent hours lying on the decking outside the conservatory. She was a very good 'mouser,' she would have put some cats to shame. Where we live we see a lot of wildlife, foxes, hedgehogs and field mice. At dusk I insisted that Siani came in and most times when I went to call her in, there would be a tiny furry body lying next to her on the decking. There was never a mark on the mouse but it was very definitely dead. My husband had the job of disposing of the body.

One day when I was at work I received a frantic telephone call from my husband who told me that he had "lost Siani." Apparently, he had let Tia and Siani out into the back garden and when he went to call them back in, he could not see Siani anywhere. He assured me that he had not opened the back gate so I knew she could not be far away. A friend and colleague had called in to see me and he agreed to stay in my office while I dashed back home. I rushed into the back garden, I called Siani's name and told her to 'speak' I heard a plaintive bark and tracked her down behind a large garden bench. I moved the bench and she was able to back out. I think she had gone on a bit of mooch about and got stuck. I gave her a cuddle and checked that she was OK and not hurt. Once I was sure that she was alright, I went back to work. How my husband failed to find her is a mystery, Men !!!

Siani and Tia

Siani and Tia really enjoyed their trips to the seaside

Tia and Siani on a beach somewhere in Wales, it was very windy but at least it wasn't raining

CHAPTER 12

Growing Old Gracefully

The girls had settled in together really well and we were all enjoying leisurely walks across the fields and along the canal tow path where we took time to watch the ducks and the swans. We took them to the seaside and Siani went to the water's edge but was a bit surprised when the edge moved and she got her feet wet, but they both enjoyed running along the beach.

Tia had always had problems with her eyes, from an early age she had suffered with dry eye syndrome. This meant putting drops of 'artificial tears' in both eyes several times a day. She then developed in-growing eyelashes, having tried several remedies, she finally had surgery which seemed to solve the problem. Some time later, her left eye became very red and looked really sore, it turned out that she had an ulcer in that eye. This meant several trips to the vet, eventually this cleared up but then she developed an ulcer on her right eye, so there were more trips to the vet. Finally, the problem cleared up but her eye sight was deteriorating and in the end it became very poor and she could barely see anything. We would be walking across the field and she would lose her bearings and not know in which direction to go, so I bought a whistle and when she got a bit lost, I would blow the whistle to get her attention and then call her to me. This seemed to work well.

In addition to her eye troubles, she also had problems with her teeth. She had lost a few and then due to chronic gum disease, the vet recommended that all her teeth be removed, which they were. She adapted to being toothless really well, for a while I only gave her soft food but it would not take long before she was eating normally again. She did look a bit strange sometimes when she was asleep, her tongue sort of lolled out of one side of her mouth.

She had also developed arthritis in both her back legs and had trouble getting up, once up she could walk slowly. Siani had been diagnosed with arthritis in her back legs some time earlier and was on daily medication. They were both still able to go for short, slow walks across the fields but that was all they wanted to do.

Not far from where we live is a rescue kennels which is part of the Birmingham Dogs' Home. We have been frequent visitors over the years, taking food and blankets for the lost and unwanted dogs there and when we first became involved with the Samoyed Rescue we made an arrangement with the Kennel Manager to let us know if they had a Samoyed in and we would re-home it through the Rescue Society.

One day one of our neighbours, who was also a frequent visitor to this kennels, came over to tell us that they had spotted a Samoyed in one of the cages. We waited for a telephone call, but none came. The next time our neighbour went, the Samoyed had gone. We assumed that the kennels had either traced the owner or tried to re-home it themselves. A few days later, however, we were told that the Samoyed was back and we did get a telephone call from the kennels.

My husband and I went to see the Sammy. He was quite small and very thin and a bit lively to say the least. He was, apparently, a bit of a Houdini and the kennels had been told by his owner that they did not want him back. We contacted the Rescue Society and it just so happened that there was a retired couple who had recently lost their Sam and were looking for another one.

It was agreed that they would take this little dog, so my husband took him up to a kennel near Nottingham to await their arrival. Before this couple could go and get the little dog, the Rescue received a telephone call to say that a five year old female Sammy was in need of a home. Her owner had died and there was no-one who could take care of her. After some discussion, it was thought that this female would suit the retired couple better, so they agreed to have her instead.

Unfortunately, this tale had a tragic twist. The husband and wife were a lovely couple and the dog settled in with them really well, they were ideally suited to each other. Sadly, the husband was involved in an accident and died instantly. The wife, obviously, was devastated but some time later, she rang the Rescue Society to say how grateful she was to have the dog, she had given her a reason to get up in the morning.

Meanwhile, this left the little dog languishing in kennels again. My husband had retired two years earlier after working in a bank for 40 years and had recently been diagnosed as 'border-line diabetic.' It was suggested that he take more exercise and since he was too old to return to playing rugby, had tried golf some years ago and did not like it much and was not a going to the gym kind of person, the easiest, and cheapest, form of exercise was walking. He asked me how I felt about taking on this little dog which would mean that we would then have three Sams.

I have to admit that I was not too keen, we live in a small house, me and my girls had settled into a quiet, leisurely routine and I was not sure that three animals together would work. On the other hand, however, I did not want to see this little dog in kennels. To our knowledge, he had been in kennels three times and had at least one home if not two. The kennels said they thought he was about three years old but I felt he was quite a bit younger. He had met 'the girls' on two occasions, but only for a few minutes and all had gone well, but that is not quite the same as all living under the same roof. I agreed to have him on the understanding that firstly, my husband took responsibility for taking him for a walk and secondly, and more importantly, he got on with the girls and did not cause them any stress. By now, Tia was 13 years old and Siani at least 14 years old, so they just wanted what they were used to, a quiet life.

Tia followed by Siani on their walk in the fields at the back of my house (my house can be seen in the background)

Tia aged 13 years
Siani aged about 14 years

CHAPTER 13

Three Is Not Such A Crowd

My husband set off to Nottingham to fetch this little dog. The dog did not appear to have a name, so we decided to call him Tsar. When they arrived back, Tsar was even smaller and thinner than I remembered and to say that he was extremely lively would be a bit of an understatement. He bounded into the house dragging my husband behind him. I had opened the doors to the garden and he rushed out there and raced around like a cheetah on speed. Tia was a little curious about this manic mutt but stayed quite close to Siani who was completely disinterested in the whole thing. He finally calmed down and came back into the lounge and jumped straight on to the window sill which was to become his favourite spot. Siani had long since given up trying to jump up there and had adopted the spot under the window as hers, Tia would sometimes lie by her there or go into the hall.

Now that Tsar was calm, Tia's curiosity got the better of her and she went up to have a closer look, I think Siani had done much to restore her confidence. He hopped down from the window sill and they rubbed noses. That went well. He thought he would do the same to Siani who was lying under the window, she gave a low, half hearted bark as he got closer to her and I wondered what he would do. I watched anxiously, but he just backed off and went into the kitchen for a drink of water, followed by Tia.

The next hurdle would be feeding three dogs in the small space that is my kitchen. Some dogs can be protective of food and I did not know how Tsar would be. Again, I need not have worried. I put the food down, the girls went to their usual positions next to each other and I put Tsar's dish on the end. He ate his food very quickly but as soon as he had finished, he came out of the kitchen, he made no effort to go to either of the other dishes although the girls were still eating.

The next morning, we prepared for our first walk of the day. Tsar was much smaller than any of our other Sams and we had not got a collar small enough for him, so my husband made what he thought was an adequate modification to the smallest one we had and we set off into the fields. The first field is divided into two by a hedge with a gap half way down to get through to the other half. At the end of this field is a cart track over that is the second field which is also divided into two by a hedge. At the bottom of this, there is a brook and a gate into the other half. Over the brook is the third field. The girls and myself went into the field first, followed by my husband and Tsar. He walked perfectly well until we got into the first field and it was as though someone had flicked a switch in his brain. Wow! Open space. Must run.

He took one look at all the space, his eyes widened, his ears pricked up, he slipped his collar and disappeared like a rat up a drainpipe. He ran at great speed straight down the first field, across the cart track and straight down the second field, over the brook into the third field and was lost from view. We were panic stricken, there was nothing we could do, we certainly could not move as fast as him. We set off after him, calling him, whistling him, I even got the girls to 'speak' in the vain hope that their bark might bring him back to us. It did not.

He reappeared from behind a hedge, we called him again, he looked at us and darted through the gate into the other half of the field and carried on running.

Fortunately, one of our fellow dog walkers was coming towards us and we yelled at him to grab the dog, which he did and managed to hang on to him until we got there. Although my girls were not on a lead, I always carried the leads with me and I managed to get one of these round his neck and we decided to head home.

The next few excursions into the fields followed much the same pattern. Tsar pulled so hard on the make-shift collar and lead that he broke it. He ran off, but this time I caught him. With a new collar and lead, we tried again, this contraption was much stronger but when he pulled on it, my husband fell over and Tsar escaped again. He was caught by a man with a black Labrador who knew us and hung on to Tsar until we got there. Then he caught my husband off guard and pulled the lead out of his hand, this time my husband's rugby training came in useful and he rugby tackled him to the ground, much to the amusement of other dog walkers who happened to be watching. He is now taken out with a collar that fits which has two separate hooks, a bit like a belt and braces situation.

Opening the front door was just as dangerous. The call 'Tsar's gone' became a common phrase. Fortunately, everyone in the village had known Zara and Max and knew Tia and Siani, so they all knew that Tsar belonged to us and he was brought back by a variety of people. We are now much more aware that we must close one door before opening another.

Even in the back garden we could not trust him, despite having six foot fences all the way round. One warm sunny day, the couple next door, their daughter and their two Springer Spaniels were having lunch in their garden when there was a sudden shriek from the daughter. She had seen a little white head appear over the top of the fence between us and thought he was coming over. The male Springer was so frightened, apparently, that he ran into the house and hid under a table. As Tsar landed, I grabbed hold of him, I think had he had a second attempt, he would have gone over. We had to watch him every minute.

In the house, however, he was really good but extremely noisy. Sitting on the window sill he could see right to the bottom of the close and anything and everything that moved was an opportunity for him to bark and he used this to full advantage. With the girls he was absolutely brilliant, he never worried or harassed them, he treated them with the greatest respect. If they were in his way, he simply jumped over them. When he was playing with the ball, if it landed near to either of the girls he was really gentle when retrieving it. We could not have had a better dog with regard to the girls if we had ordered one specially. He was also very affectionate with us, so why he wanted to run off was a mystery.

20.04.2006 1

Tsar on a visit before we decided to keep him. Tsar is on the kennel lead, next to him is Siani, then Tia

Tsar when he first came to live with us, aged, we think, about
18 months

CHAPTER 14

Three, Two, One

Tsar did calm down quite a bit. The kennels said that they thought he was about three years old, but a couple of friends of ours who had been around Sams for many years agreed with me and thought he was about eighteen months old. We had him castrated just in case he escaped and we could not catch him before he got into some sort of mischief. The last thing we wanted was a paternity suit ! His weight doubled which served two purposes, firstly he looked a lot healthier and secondly, he could not jump quite so high, or get through small gaps so easily.

He came upstairs at bed time and slept on the bed with us. Tia had always slept on the bed, but just before we had Tsar, she could just about still manage to get up the stairs but had given up trying to jump on the bed and instead, slept on the floor on my side of the bed. Eventually, she stopped coming upstairs altogether and spent all night and most of the day lying at the bottom of the stairs. We all got used to stepping over her when going up or coming down the stairs. Siani spent most of her time now lying under the window by the television. The health of both of the girls was deteriorating.

Siani gave up going for a walk, it was all she could do to go out into the garden. She could only get up with our help and had trouble walking. She was so brave, she never moaned or complained and she tried so hard to get up on her own. She gave up eating her food which was a real worry. I used to take her food to her in the lounge and get down on the floor and spoon feed her. When she stopped eating that I tried feeding her soup, which worked for a while. When I lost Max, I made a promise to myself that I would never keep a dog alive for selfish reasons just because I could not let go and here I was doing it again. As I watched her drag herself across the lounge, I knew that I could not let this go on. I rang the vet. As my husband lifted her into the car, we knew that we would not be bringing her home. The vet came out to the car and they lifted her on to a stretcher and took her into a side room. Again, I took the coward's way out and as my husband went in with her, I sat on the wall outside the surgery in floods of tears.

We drove home in silence, I had lost my lovely Siani, a quiet, gentle soul, who had never asked for or expected anything from me. I would like to think that the last ten years of her life had been much better than the first six or eight. Tia was asleep when we left and she was in the same position when we returned, I am not sure that she even knew we had been out or that Siani was not there. Tsar, instead of meeting us in the hall with a toy in his mouth, which was the usual greeting, he was just sitting on the window sill. I think he knew that something was not quite right.

Tia eventually woke up and walked slowly into the lounge, she looked at the spot where Siani usually lay, then she looked around the lounge. Alongside the fire place I have a half life sized model of a Samoyed, Tia went up to this and pushed it with her nose and was very confused when she did not get a response from it. She went into the kitchen, she went into the garden, came back in and looked around the lounge again. She was obviously a bit bewildered. Eventually, she went back into the hall and lay down at the bottom of the stairs.

Misty eyed, I washed Siani's dish and put it into the garage. I moved Tia's dish to the corner by the sink and put Tsar's dish by the cooker. My husband took Tsar for a walk, Tia did not want to go, so while she slept, I cried again. I was not sure which of the girls would go first but I knew that once one of them had gone, the other would not be far behind.

Tia had no teeth, could see almost nothing and needed help getting up. Some days she could walk a short distance but was having trouble getting up and down the three steps at the bottom of the garden, so most of the time she just pottered around the garden. Every morning when I came downstairs, I had to look really closely to see if she was still breathing.

One morning she cried as I tried to help her to stand up, when she stood up, she yelped and flopped back down. Something was seriously wrong. I rang the vet and we took her down immediately. Somehow, again, I think I just knew that we would not be bringing her home. The vet came out to the car because Tia could not stand up, he checked her legs and told us that she had dislocated her hip. He also said that her breathing was very shallow and he could barely find a pulse. Then I heard those words again "the kindest thing ……."

My husband and I just looked at each other and nodded. By now I was totally distraught, I was still getting over the death of Siani and now I was going to lose my little princess. Through a veil of tears, I watched as my husband, the vet and Tia disappeared into the same side room that Siani had been taken into four months previously. It was only recently, when I was looking through some paper work, that I realised that Tia had died on the same date as Max, ten years apart. Max was the love of Tia's life, strange coincidence.

Poor little Tsar must have wondered what kind of home he had ended up in. He started out having two girls to watch over, then he had one, then he had none.

I think we always knew that we would continue with the tradition of having two Sammies but because during his short life, Tsar had been through enough disruption having been in kennels at least three times and been in probably two homes, I desperately wanted to make sure that whatever Sammy we took on would treat him with the same degree of respect and understanding that he had demonstrated with the girls. We would see what Sammies the Rescue Society had awaiting new homes and try to make the right decision from there.

'Tsar sitting with 'the girls'
Tia is on the left, Siani on the right

Tsar, Tia and Siani all very relaxed with each other

Tia and Siani, friends to the end

Poor little Tsar left all on his own

CHAPTER 15

A Single Sammy

I missed my girls dreadfully. Tia had been a big part of my life for 15 years, Siani for ten. Tia lay at the bottom of the stairs and we got used to stepping over her, Siani lay under the window so whenever I sat down to watch the television she was in my peripheral vision. Now there were just empty spaces. Obviously, our friends knew that I had lost my girls and word spread quickly. I was amazed at the response I got from everyone, people in the village would stop me to say how sorry they were to hear the news, I received numerous emails and telephone calls and a couple of 'sorry for your loss' cards, one from my niece in America.

My husband continued to take Tsar out for his walks, sometimes I would go with them but mostly I did not, it was just not the same. Tia, then Tsar, had been frequent visitors to a residential care home where my husband's aunt lived. There were also a few residents there who used to live in the village. The residents loved to see the dogs and if my husband went without them, they all asked where they were, so he would put Tsar in his car and go off with him. This left me completely alone and made me miss my girls even more.

We had notified the Rescue Society when we lost Siani and then again when we lost Tia, this time I had said that I would be prepared now to take another Sammy. Although Tsar had not appeared to be that close to the girls, he did seem to miss them. He now jumped over the space where they used to be as though they were still there. Feeding three dogs in my small kitchen was a bit of a squeeze, now I was down to one

I decided to move Tsar's dish to where Tia used to eat because there was more room there. The first time I put his tea down after we lost Tia, he refused to go anywhere near it and just kept looking up at me. No amount of pointing to the dish or trying to coax him towards it did any good, he just looked at me as if to say that is where Tia eats. I eventually moved his dish back to his usual spot and he immediately started to eat, so that is where it stayed.

Sometimes he would lie quietly in the lounge but mostly he wanted to play ball and would bring it to me and push it at me if I ignored him. If I was trying to read the paper, he would put his paw on the top of the paper and knock it out of my hand to let me know he was there and wanted to play. If it was not a ball, it would be a rope thing with which he liked to play tug of war. He also liked to rush up and down the garden barking at any pigeon or black bird who had the audacity to perch on our fence. He would also bark furiously at helicopters telling them not to land in his back garden, this strategy obviously worked as we have not yet had a helicopter land in the garden, we did, however, have a hot air balloon crash land in one of the fields at the back of the house, fortunately, no-one was hurt.

When I rang the Rescue Society, I did not make any specific requests for the kind of Sam I wanted because I really did not know what to say. Did I want a male or female, a young Sammy, I had forgotten quite how energetic young Sams were and how much they pulled on the lead, or did I want an older Sam, quieter and more sedate. I thought I would just let fate take a hand and see what happened, but I think I really wanted an older Sam as most of my get up and go and got up and gone.

After about three weeks, the Rescue Society rang to say that there was an older female Sam in need of a home. As with a lot of rescue dogs, the story was a bit convoluted, but the end result was that this Sammy needed a new home.

It was suggested that we contact the owners direct to see if they would be prepared to meet us half way, as where they lived was quite a long drive for us. They said that they would and we agreed to meet at a pub, a journey of one hour for them and two hours for us. We arrived at the pub about fifteen minutes early and waited. The appointed time came and went, so did a further thirty minutes. We wondered if they had changed their minds as they had, apparently, had this dog a long time. After another thirty minutes, I remembered that they had given us a mobile telephone number, so I rang them. It seemed that there had been a very bad car accident and they were stuck in a traffic jam. They could actually see the pub from their car but could just not get to it. They rang us about ten minutes later to say that the traffic had started moving and they would be with us very soon.

We saw them arrive and went out to the car park to meet them. They seemed like a really nice couple and the Sammy, who was called Misty, was quiet and friendly, but she was a big girl, similar in size to Zara and Max and twice the size of little Tsar. Nonetheless, Tsar and Misty greeted each other, not a word was spoken by either of them but the tails were wagging enthusiastically. We thought that the two of them would get on, so we agreed to take her. We set off on our journey home with the newest member of our family.

Tsar in his favourite spot

The view of Tsar that greets everyone who comes into the Close

If they get too close to the house, he stands up!

How Tsar likes to sleep sometimes

CHAPTER 16

The Sixth Sam

We arrived home safely. We had put Tsar on the back seat and Misty in the back of the car. Tsar jumped out of the car, I hung on to his lead while my husband lifted Misty out of the back, Tsar dragged me into the house and Misty walked in slowly behind us. She went straight into the kitchen and had a drink, then she barked to go out, we let her out into the back garden and she went and lay down on the paving slabs outside the conservatory, where she seemed happy to stay.

We all went for a walk, she was excellent on a lead, she did not pull at all, she just plodded along by my side all round the field. We met a few of the regular dogs and owners who all wanted to meet our new arrival but she did not seem overly bothered. She really just seemed resigned to whatever fate had in store for her, a bit like Siani when we first had her. She also looked older than her years, we had been told that she was between eight and a half and nine years old.

I had noticed that after she had walked only a few steps, her legs seemed to give way and she flopped down. I could understand this happening whilst going round the fields as the ground was quite uneven and there were many enormous mole hills, looking at the height and diameter of these mole hills, the moles must be the size of Labradors, but it also happened when she walked across the lounge carpet. This gave me cause for concern so when we took her to our vet for a check up, as we have done with all our Sams, I mentioned this. They did not give any explanation except to say that there were signs of arthritis and she was very overweight, but apart from that, she seemed to be healthy.

One other thing bothered me, all night long she moaned. When we came down to her on several occasions throughout the night, she seemed to be asleep, so maybe she was dreaming as she did not seem to be in any physical distress.

A few weeks after we had her, we took her to a Pets and People show at another stately home near to where we live. It was there that I made the best purchase ever. Misty was still very reluctant to spend time in the house and much preferred to stay outside but I did not like the idea of her lying on the paving slabs. At one of the stalls, I found a mesh bed on metal legs, which I thought would be ideal for Misty when she was outside. I bought the largest size they did and she could just about fit on it. When we got home, we put it in her favourite spot and tried to get her to lie on it but she would not have anything to do with it. Instead, she tried to squeeze into the very small gap between the fence and her new bed. Is white the equivalent of blonde in the animal world? I was beginning to think that I had just wasted fifty pounds. We continued to coax her on to it and finally she climbed on. Since then, we have had trouble getting her off it, even when it is going dark, she will not come in and I used to have to get her lead and practically drag her off it. Now, however, she will come in when I call her, well, most of the time.

After our initial visit to the vet. I started to monitor her food intake, she did still get the odd treat, including a small piece of pork pie occasionally and small bits of cheese. She even seemed to look forward to going for a walk, when I picked up her lead, she barked continuously until we got into the field. She even seemed pleased to meet other dogs and their owners. Gradually, the moaning during the night stopped and she started to lose weight. I am told by a former member of a rambling club that if we walk round the perimeter of three of the fields, the distance is about two miles. We were doing this twice a day and I think this was helping in Misty's weight loss. She has now lost just under a stone in the eleven months we have had her and looks and moves much better for it.

We were told that the only thing she would play with was a tennis ball. There was already a box full of assorted toys and I thought she would simply find one of those she liked and play with that. She did go to the toy box, picked a few items out of it, discarded them and walked away in disgust. I relented and went out and bought a pack of five tennis balls. I gave one to her, she bit into it and split it in half. She did the same thing with the other four. I gave up on tennis balls but I did buy two hard, sponge balls and gave her one of those. That she seemed to like, but she had not quite grasped the concept of me throwing the ball and her fetching it. In fact, it was quite the opposite.

The first time she picked up the ball and then dropped it, I picked it up and threw it across the room. She looked at me, then at the ball, then at me again with a look on her face that indicated that she thought I had gone completely mad. I got up, fetched the ball and rolled it across the floor to her. She picked the ball up and dropped it on the floor, where it rolled a little way from where she was standing. She stood there while I got up, fetched the ball and rolled it back to her. This was the way it continued, good game!

Tsar was exactly the opposite, he would bring the ball to me and I would throw it, he would chase it, pick it up and run back for me to throw it again. He would leap in the air to catch it, he would be really good at fly ball, or he would dribble it along the floor, his footwork was brilliant, I am sure that if I could find him some little boots, he would get a game with a well known premier league football team.

When Tsar played with the toys, he was very careful to avoid Tia and Siani and now Misty, he was also very good at avoiding the ornaments. One day I was in the bedroom and Tsar was sitting on the bed, when I heard an almighty crash, I rushed down the stairs to find the half life size model of a Sam, which had stood by the side of the fireplace for twenty odd years, was now in three pieces. Poor Misty, the noise of the crash must have given her a bit of a fright. Fortunately, my husband is very good with a pot of glue and managed to put it back together again and unless you look really closely, you would never know that it had been involved in an accident.

After only a few weeks of having Misty, I felt confident enough to take her round the fields without her lead on. She was fairly obedient but more importantly I knew that she would not run off, unlike Tsar, who, if we had let him off the lead, would have gone off like a rocket. Most of the dogs in the field were off the lead, the younger ones would race about chasing each other and bowling each other over, the older dogs would amble around and sniff a lot, mole hills seemed to be of particular interest. This worked really well until one day in December. Over night we had a heavy fall of snow and the next morning everywhere was frozen solid. We took the dogs out as usual, Misty does a lot of sniffing whilst Tsar just wants to get on with his walk, as a consequence, he is much further ahead of us. This particular morning, Misty decided, in order to catch up with Tsar, she would not go round the path on the edge of the field but would take a short cut across the middle of the field. She started to bound across, I was running behind her trying to stay upright, look where I was going and keep an eye on her.

When I looked up, she was flat on the grass, when I got to her she was not moving. My husband met me in the middle of the field, we called her name but got no response, I lifted her head and it just flopped back down. I really thought she had broken her neck. By now, two other dog walkers had come to see what was wrong, we just watched her for another minute but there was still no response. I took Tsar home and grabbed a tarpaulin and ran back to the field. By this time, quite a crowd had formed around Misty, which was fortunate because we had to roll her on to the tarpaulin and it took four men to carry her back to our house and put her in the back of my husband's car. In the meantime, I had rung our vet, explained what had happened and they had told us to take her straight down.

When we got there, the vet came out to the car as she had still not quite 'come round' Between us we managed to get her to sit up and then on to the floor, she then walked into the surgery but she was still very wobbly. The vet said that he did not think there were any broken bones but she was still very dazed. He gave her an injection and some tablets to take for the next few days. We were also told that for the next week we must keep her on a lead and only walk her in the garden. It was not long, however, before she was back to normal and there did not seem to be any permanent damage.

It was around this time that we received a telephone call from a woman who had just found her uncle dead in his chair. His wife had died a week previously. A few years ago, the Rescue had placed a Samoyed with this couple and because it was in our area, my husband had kept in touch with them. When his wife died, the man contacted us and asked us to promise that we would find a good home for this dog should anything happen to him. He had also told his niece and that is why she rang us. My husband immediately went over and picked the dog up. In the meantime, I contacted the Rescue to tell them what had happened. Fortunately, they had a home suitable for this dog. As it was quite late at night when we got the call, we kept the dog overnight. She was a sweet little dog, aged about eight years and she got on well with Misty and Tsar. Although she had been much loved, she had not been groomed for a while, so the following morning my husband took her up to a kennels in Nottingham so that she could be groomed ready for her new home. The last we heard was that she had gone to her new home and had settled in well.

Misty when she first came to us aged, we think, about 9 years

Misty outside on her bed

Even the snow did not put her off

CHAPTER 17

The Final Chapter

Over the last 27 years, I have lived with six Sammies. My friends all said that they could not tell the difference between any of them because, they said, they all looked the same and I suppose, from a distance, they did. They were also quite similar in other ways. Zara and Tia looked very much alike although Tia was only half the size of Zara. Both their coats were thick but their fur was soft and silky. They were both very definitely indoor, house dogs and were very comfortable in a home environment. They both expected, as their right, to sleep on our bed and sit on our furniture downstairs, which, of course, we allowed them to do. They both very much resented being left alone and they showed their resentment by being destructive. They were both very affectionate and enjoyed being hugged. They demanded attention and got it in bucket loads, not just from us but from everyone they met. The only difference was that Zara was a carer and Tia needed to be cared for.

Max and Siani were also quite alike, although again, Siani was only half the size of Max. Both their coats were really thick but their fur was much coarser   Neither of them seemed to be comfortable being in a house. They were never happy being on the bed or on the furniture, they knew their place and that was on the floor, except that sometimes Siani preferred the window sill. It seemed that both of them always had to be by a door. Although most nights they started off lying in the hall, a lot of times they would end up sleeping in the utility room. They never seemed to mind us leaving them and they never did any real damage, although Max did tear up the mail for a couple of days until we fixed a tray under the letter box. Neither of them sought attention or affection, I think perhaps they had never had much of either, except, perhaps, the wrong sort of attention. As a consequence, they were really not sure what to make of the hugging business, but, eventually, they learned to put up with it.

Misty looks a bit like Zara and is about the same size. She has a similar coat to Siani and will tolerate being brushed although she is not very keen. It is not long before I find myself chasing her around the lounge. She has been upstairs to the bedroom once but did not stay very long. She has never made any attempt to get on the furniture. She much prefers to be outside and, like Max and Siani, although she starts the night in the hall, she ends up in the utility room. She never really craves attention or affection but she is getting used to being hugged.

Tsar is a bit of a mixture of all of them. He is even smaller than Tia and Siani and although he has more fur now than when we first got him, his coat is nowhere near as thick as any of the others. He absolutely hates being brushed. He is very affectionate and often comes over just for a cuddle. He curls up on the bed but has never made any attempt to get on the furniture downstairs, he much prefers the window sill. He has a really sweet nature and treats Misty with the same degree of care that he demonstrated with 'the girls.'

The one thing they all have in common is a hatred of being brushed. In between their professional grooming, I did try to brush them myself. Zara was a big dog, Max had only three good legs, Tia and Siani both had arthritis yet all of them could move at the speed of light when they saw me with a brush in my hand. How I managed to collect enough fur for a skirt and jacket still amazes me.

In a couple of month's time, we will have had Tsar for three years and Misty for one year. That makes Tsar about four and half years old and Misty, we think, about ten years old.

Misty (who most of the time I call Misty Wisty) has now settled in well. She still likes to be outside, but at least she will now use her bed. At night she has decided to start off sleeping in the hall and mostly she lies on her back with her feet in the air or on her side stretched out so that she takes up almost all the room in the hall way. I have noticed, lately however, that when I come down in the morning, she is asleep in the utility room. She still moans a bit but certainly not as much as she did. She loves her walks but most of the time I keep her on a lead because I am so worried that she will break into a gallop and fall over again. If I meet up with a couple of the regular dog walkers with older dogs, I will take Misty's lead off and let her walk around with them. At the start of the walk, she will trot round the field and I can just about keep up with her, as the walk progresses, she slows down a bit. If I have to keep the lead on her, she does not seem to mind too much and, like Siani, she does not pull me around, unlike Zara, Max, Tia and Tsar. Thinking about it though, perhaps it is because she is older, when Zara, Max and Tia got older, they stopped pulling on the lead and became a joy to take for a walk.

Misty is an affectionate, gentle old soul and has got used to me putting my arms around her neck and hugging her, as I have done with all our previous Sams. She gets on well with Tsar but she will try to steal his tea if she finishes eating before him, but if I tell her to leave it, she will. She is a bit of a thief though, if we leave the rubbish bag on the floor, she will go into it to see what she can find. One of my husband's

98

dog walking jackets has zip pockets and there is always biscuits in them. If he leaves his jacket on the chair in the lounge over night, in the morning the pockets are soggy and the biscuits reduced to crumbs. Misty must go mooching during the night but has not yet mastered the art of opening the zip. It may only be a matter of time !

Tsar (who most of the time I call Tsarzie) is very affectionate and really enjoys being hugged. He comes on to the bed at night but usually ends up on the floor by the bedroom door. Sometimes he lies flat on his back with his feet in the air, but most of the time he curls himself into a ball and covers his nose with his tail. He is also very gentle and when Misty goes towards his dish, even though he has not finished eating, he will back off and let her have the remainder of the food. He is, however, very noisy, he barks at anything that moves in the close, including other dogs. He used to bark at all the dogs he saw in the fields, but now he has got to know them, he is much better and quieter. He doesn't seem to mind too much being left in the house although he does bark quite a bit when we leave but he has never done any damage. He still has the odd manic moment, however, when he rushes up and down the stairs and around the lounge playing football.

He is also a howler, the first one we have had. Max used to 'sing' to the theme music to an Australian soap opera but at least he was almost in tune. Tsar just throws his head back and howls. He particularly likes (or dislikes ?) the theme tunes to a couple of my favourite television programmes plus several adverts. The other day I was watching a programme on television when they played, as background music, the song Who Let the Dogs Out, he loved that ! He has always been an inside dog and shown no desire to go outside for any length of time, except for a walk It is particularly hard to get him to go out when it is raining. Now, however, if Misty is outside on her bed, he will go and lie on the decking by her.

Unfortunately, his barking and howling have not gone unnoticed, our neighbours of nearly forty years, told us the other day (in the nicest possible way) that he was certainly the noisiest Sam we had ever had.

Over the years, many Samoyeds have drifted in and out of my life and I absolutely love the breed. I can not imagine having any other breed of dog, which is fortunate because I have over 100 models of Sammies all over the house.

I think I am a bit of a hoarder/collector. My first collection was models of hedgehogs, this was because we had a hedgehog as a frequent visitor in our garden and my mum bought me my first hedgehog model. That started me off and over a few years I collected about 150. Just after we had Zara, I noticed a model of a Sam at one of our local markets and I just had to buy it. That started my collection of Sammy models which just seemed to grow. I was running out of space so I decided my hedgehog collection would have to go.

I had heard about an animal hospital in Buckinghamshire, which although synonymous with hedgehogs, also looked after a variety of injured wild animals and birds. I decided to donate my hedgehog collection to this hospital. This left room for more Sammy models. I now have over a hundred and apart from the usual ceramic/stonecast/metal models, I have three made from glass and five figurines each with a Sam, three of which are made by a well known Potteries manufacturer, these are amongst my favourites of all the models in my collection. I also collect dog money boxes and enjoy going round antiques fairs trying to find ones that I have not already got, which is proving quite difficult now that I have almost a hundred of those. I also have a large collection of pictures of dogs, one has the caption 'the more I know about people, the more I like my dogs.' This one I particularly like.

All the Samoyeds I have met over the years have been full of character and personality, some of them indulge in 'growl talk' and if you are not familiar with this, it can be a bit off putting. I never heard either Zara or Siani growl, ever. Tia grumbled a bit when asked to give up a bit of space on the bed and Misty 'talks' loudly to herself quite a lot. The biggest exponent of 'growl talk' though is Tsar. He will bring a toy over to me and place it on the floor, he will then stand over it and invite me to try to pick it up before he can. If I move towards it, he growls and if you do not understand the tone, you would be very reluctant to go anywhere near the subject toy, but I know he would never hurt me intentionally. Max, however, was a different story, when he growled, he meant it. It was a definite warning to stay away from him, believe me, you can tell the difference. He may, however, have had a valid reason and I would never judge him for that. Anyway, in the end he was fine and became a good example of the breed.

Whilst I love the breed, the Samoyed is not for everyone. That cute bundle of white fluff grows into a big, strong dog. Although it now comes into the Pastoral group, the Samoyed is a working breed and, as such, needs a lot of exercise. They are intelligent and need constant brain stimulation. They are sociable, love people and hate being left alone. They need constant grooming, which can be hard work and they moult a lot. They can be wilful and difficult to train. They can be particularly vociferous, which may not go down too well with neighbours.

Despite the destruction and subsequent expense, the barking, the pulling on the lead, the high maintenance grooming regime and the never ending moulting, I do not have a single moment of regret in choosing the Samoyed.

So, if you can put up with all that stuff, have the time to groom and walk them, spend time with them, have a sense of humour and infinite patience and are not overly house proud, the Samoyed is a loyal and faithful friend. They are friendly, affectionate and very huggable. They are happy souls and always seem to be smiling. On the whole, the Samoyed is an absolute joy to be around. In fact, it is Always a Pleasure.

I will always be grateful to the Samoyed Rescue for Max, Siani, Tsar and Misty and to our fellow British Samoyed Club committee member who was happy for us to give Tia a home and to the woman down south from whom we got Zara.

I also have tremendous admiration for all those people who devote their time to taking care of injured and unwanted animals. I just wish that all dogs, in fact all animals, could be treated with kindness and respect and live safe and happy lives, free from pain and suffering.

Tsar and Misty in the garden when Misty first came to us

Tsar and Misty have become good friends

Tsar and Misty in the back garden enjoying the snow

Three of my favourite figurines. The two little models are Sammies, one dressed as an angel, the other a devil. Says it all !!

The large pot model before it met Misty

Tsar as he is now (May 2009)
He is still quite lively and full of character, and since he hasn't made a mad dash for freedom lately, I think he has decided to stay with us.

Misty as she is now (May 2009)
She is a gentle old soul who has settled in well and seems happy to be with us.

THE VERSE

Just after we had Zara, I went through a bit of a phase where I tried writing verse, mostly for friends and various occasions. I decided to write one about Zara and Max, it went something like this :

My Beautiful Samoyeds

My beautiful Samoyeds, Zara and Max
Are lovely in so many ways
Apart, that is, for one or two facts
About how they spend most of their days

When we went out to work, Zara would fret
And get herself into a state
So after a bit of a chat with our vet
We decided to get her a mate

When Max first arrived he was so thin and scared
He came through the rescue, you see
Obtained from some people who just never cared
I'm so glad that he came to me

Zara, by then, we'd had for three years
She'd established her home here with us
She did a great deal to allay Max's fears
And he settled without too much fuss

I don't think his life had held many joys
But still he seemed anxious to please
Zara was happy to share all her toys
And introduced him to ice cream and cheese

Of each other they quickly became very fond
And hated being apart
It was clear from the start there was a very strong bond
With a love that came right from the heart

Before we had Sams I had heard the rumour
That they could be naughty but nice
If I'd known the extent of their sense of humour
I really might just have thought twice

At night when I'm sleeping they're plotting away
Smiling about what they will do
As soon as I've gone out to work for the day
I wonder this time what they'll chew

They've a box full of toys and bones and balls
But there is something they like even more
Such as stripping the wallpaper off the hall walls
And scattering it all over the floor

They've dug up the carpet and shredded newspapers
They have taken books off the shelves
It's really enough to give one the vapours
But they seem to enjoy themselves

They've chewed up a camera and numerous shoes
And a couple of five pound notes
Have tried very hard to open bottles of booze
And ripped out the pockets in coats

They chewed up the TV remote control
And a cheque that came through the post
But the middle of a toilet roll
Is what they enjoy the most

They both have a nose for edible things
And one day they raided the larder
So we tied up the door with pieces of string
But this made them try even harder

They ate two Christmas puds and a packet of rice
Some bread off the kitchen table
They tried a tin of tomatoes but that wasn't nice
So they gave up and just ate the label

One year they ate all my Christmas chocs
Which put me in a bit of a spot
They ate all my liqueurs, even the box
Next day Zara's eyes were bloodshot

They're fed on fresh chicken and top side of beef
Which would put some humans to shame
So why do they cause me all this much grief
Do you think my cooking's to blame

We go for a walk every night after work
As I slip the lead over his head
Max gets so excited and goes quite beserk
And his bark would waken the dead

Keeping control is a bit of a fight
It's amusing and makes people talk
I'm trying my best with all of my might
Then folks yell "who's taking who for a walk"

Max is so proud of his singing voice
He watches TV every day
He certainly has impeccable choice
He sings to Neighbours and Home and Away

Zara can't stand the comb and the brush
Oh please don't brush me she begs
But I lie her down to a deathly hush
Then she seems to grow four extra legs

Their fur is so soft and they moult all the time
As I'm sure we are all well aware
To throw it away seemed a bit of a crime
So I started to save all their hair

I was really quite pleased with my jacket and skirt
And when I wore it I felt rather grand
But when it starts to show the first signs of dirt
Is it dry clean, machine wash or hand

Zara is ten, Max is seven in May
And to change their ways they're too old
But I just wouldn't have them any other way
To me they're more precious than gold

The joy they have brought me I just cannot measure
They are charming and cheerful and clever
And to so many others they have given much pleasure
I will love them for ever and ever.

About the Author

The author was born in 1947 during one of the most severe winters and heaviest snow falls on record.

As a child, she lived on a farm with her parents and maternal grandfather.

On leaving school, she got a job as a secretary with a precision engineering company that manufactured aircraft components. Having completed 45 years unbroken service, she retired in June 2007.

In 1970 she got married and moved to a delightful village in South Staffordshire, where she still lives with her husband and two dogs. Samoyeds of course!

CPSIA information can be obtained
at www.ICGtesting.com
Printed in the USA
LVIW012356170812

2973LVUK00002B